Contents

DOBERGE CAKE 3
NO-BAKE GREEK YOGURT CHEESECAKE 8
THE REAL RED VELVET CAKE.. 9
CHANTAL'S NEW YORK CHEESECAKE 10
CARROT CAKE 10
DOUBLE LAYER PUMPKIN CHEESECAKE 11
SIMPLE WHITE CAKE 12
ONE BOWL CHOCOLATE CAKE 13
WHITE CHOCOLATE RASPBERRY CHEESECAKE 13
SAM'S FAMOUS CARROT CAKE 14
EXTREME CHOCOLATE CAKE 15
BLACK MAGIC CAKE 16
BANANA CAKE 17
SOPAPILLA CHEESECAKE PIE 18
CAKE BALLS 18
TIRAMISU LAYER CAKE 19
GOLDEN RUM CAKE 20
BEST CARROT CAKE EVER 21
DAVID'S YELLOW CAKE 22
DARK CHOCOLATE CAKE 22
CHOCOLATE CAVITY MAKER CAKE 23
CREAM CHEESE POUND CAKE 23
RED VELVET CUPCAKES 24
CHOCOLATE CUPCAKES 25
GRANNY KAT'S PUMPKIN ROLL 26
FAVORITE OLD FASHIONED GINGERBREAD 27
BLUEBERRY SOUR CREAM COFFEE CAKE 27
BETTER THAN SEX CAKE 28
MICROWAVE CHOCOLATE MUG CAKE 29
KENTUCKY BUTTER CAKE 29
IRISH CREAM BUNDT CAKE 30
STRAWBERRY CAKE FROM SCRATCH 31
MINI CHEESECAKES 32

AWESOME CARROT CAKE WITH CREAM CHEESE FROSTING	32
ECLAIR CAKE	33
HONEY BUN CAKE	34
CHOCOLATE LOVERS' FAVORITE CAKE	34
COCONUT POKE CAKE	35
PUMPKIN CAKE	36
PEACH COBBLER DUMP CAKE	36
AUTUMN CHEESECAKE	37
WHITE ALMOND WEDDING CAKE	38
HEAVENLY WHITE CAKE	38
PUMPKIN GINGER CUPCAKES	39
AUNT ANNE'S COFFEE CAKE	40
CHOCOLATE ZUCCHINI CAKE	41
PINEAPPLE UPSIDE-DOWN CAKE	41
VEGAN CHOCOLATE CAKE	42
A-NUMBER-1 BANANA CAKE	43
GARBANZO BEAN CHOCOLATE CAKE (GLUTEN FREE!)	43
GERMAN CHOCOLATE CAKE	44
ORANGE CAKE	45
MARBLED PUMPKIN CHEESECAKE	46
BLACK BOTTOM CUPCAKES	47
FRESH STRAWBERRY UPSIDE DOWN CAKE	47
STREUSEL TOPPED BLUEBERRY MUFFINS	48
AMAZING PECAN COFFEE CAKE	49
SOUR CREAM COFFEE CAKE	50
CARROT CAKE	51
TEXAS SHEET CAKE	52
CHEESECAKE SUPREME	53
CAKE MIXES FROM SCRATCH AND VARIATIONS	53
FLOURLESS CHOCOLATE CAKE	54
SOPAPILLA CHEESECAKE DESSERT	55
BUTTERMILK POUND CAKE	56
MANDARIN ORANGE CAKE	56
DARK CHOCOLATE CAKE	57
BLUEBERRY COFFEE CAKE	58

CARROT PINEAPPLE CAKE	58
PINEAPPLE UPSIDE-DOWN CAKE	59
IRISH CREAM CHOCOLATE CHEESECAKE	60
CINNAMON SWIRL BUNDT COFFEE CAKE	61
OMA'S RHUBARB CAKE	62
GA PEACH POUND CAKE	62
GRANDMOTHER'S POUND CAKE	63
MINI CHEESECAKES	64
RED VELVET CAKE	64
PINEAPPLE UPSIDE-DOWN CAKE	65
IRISH CREAM CHOCOLATE CHEESECAKE	66
CINNAMON SWIRL BUNDT COFFEE CAKE	67
OMA'S RHUBARB CAKE	68
GA PEACH POUND CAKE	69
PUMPKIN SPICE CUPCAKES	69
CARROT CUPCAKES WITH WHITE CHOCOLATE CREAM CHEESE ICING	70
PUMPKIN CRUMB CAKE	71
COCONUT CREAM CAKE	72
LEMON CUPCAKES	73
NO-BAKE CHOCOLATE ECLAIR CAKE	74
BROWNIE CARAMEL CHEESECAKE	75
STRAWBERRY SHORTCAKE	75
TWO INGREDIENT PUMPKIN CAKE	76
EGGNOG CHEESECAKE	77
CARAMEL MACCHIATO CHEESECAKE	77
LEMON CAKE WITH LEMON FILLING AND LEMON BUTTER FROSTING	78
MINI CHEESECAKES	80
APPLE CINNAMON WHITE CAKE	80
ANGEL FOOD CAKE	81
ITALIAN CREAM CHEESE AND RICOTTA CHEESECAKE	82
CHOCOLATE COOKIE CHEESECAKE	82
CREAM FILLED CUPCAKES	83
PUMPKIN CRUNCH CAKE	84
OLD FASHIONED PINEAPPLE UPSIDE-DOWN CAKE	85
APPLE COFFEE CAKE	86

CHOCOLATE SURPRISE CUPCAKES 87

CHOCOLATE CAPPUCCINO CHEESECAKE 88

LEMON-BUTTERMILK POUND CAKE WITH AUNT EVELYN'S LEMON GLAZ 89

MELT IN YOUR MOUTH BLUEBERRY CAKE 90

FUDGE TRUFFLE CHEESECAKE 91

PUMPKIN ROLL 91

MOIST RED VELVET CUPCAKES 92

APPLE BANANA CUPCAKES 93

VEGAN CUPCAKES 94

SCRUMPTIOUS STRAWBERRY SHORTCAKE 94

BEST MOIST CHOCOLATE CAKE 95

MARGARITA CAKE 96

INCREDIBLY DELICIOUS ITALIAN CREAM CAKE 96

CHOCOLATE PUDDING FUDGE CAKE 97

BLUEBERRY POUND CAKE 98

PUMPKIN ROLL 99

CHEESE CAKE CUPS 100

LEMON CAKE 100

APPLE HARVEST POUND CAKE WITH CARAMEL GLAZE 101

WHITE TEXAS SHEET CAKE 102

THE BEST UNBAKED CHERRY CHEESECAKE EVER 103

BANANA PUDDING CAKE 103

APPLE BUNDT CAKE 104

AUNT JOHNNIE'S POUND CAKE 105

BUCHE DE NOEL 105

CHERRY CHEESECAKE 106

PUMPKIN MUFFINS WITH STREUSEL TOPPING 107

COCONUT CREAM POUND CAKE 108

SURPRISE BANANA CAKE 108

RASPBERRY ALMOND COFFEECAKE 109

TIRAMISU CHEESECAKE 110

MOIST CARROT CAKE 111

TRES LECHES CAKE 111

PEANUT BUTTER CUPCAKES 112

MARDI GRAS KING CAKE 113

CHOCOLATE POUND CAKE 114

PLUM BLUEBERRY UPSIDE DOWN CAKE 115

PECAN SOUR CREAM POUND CAKE..116

LEMON BUNDT CAKE 117

MINI CHEESECAKES WITH VANILLA WAFERS 117

AMARETTO CAKE..118

CHOCOLATE CAKE 118

PEANUT BUTTER CAKE 119

APPLE CAKE..120

OREO COOKIE CAKE 120

DOUBLE CHOCOLATE BROWNIE CAKE 121

FRESH PINEAPPLE UPSIDE DOWN CAKE 122

DOBERGE CAKE

Servings: 16 | Prep: 1h | Cooks: 25m | Total: 3h25m | Additional: 2h

NUTRITION FACTS

Calories: 917 | Carbohydrates: 125g | Fat: 45g | Protein: 11.3g | Cholesterol: 185mg

INGREDIENTS

- 4 eggs, separated
- 2 (1 ounce) squares bittersweet chocolate, chopped
- 3 1/2 cups sifted cake flour
- 4 large eggs, beaten
- 1 tablespoon baking powder
- 4 cups whole milk
- 3/4 cup butter, room temperature
- 1 tablespoon butter, room temperature
- 2 cups white sugar
- 1 tablespoon vanilla extract
- 1/2 teaspoon salt
- 1 cup butter, softened
- 1 cup milk, room temperature
- 3 cups confectioners' sugar, sifted
- 1 teaspoon lemon juice
- 1 cup unsweetened cocoa powder, sifted
- 1 teaspoon vanilla extract
- 1 teaspoon vanilla extract
- 2 cups white sugar, divided
- 1 tablespoon hot water (optional)
- 1/2 teaspoon salt
- 2 cups semisweet chocolate chips
- 1/4 cup all-purpose flour
- 2 cups heavy whipping cream
- 1/4 cup cornstarch
- 2 teaspoons vanilla extract
- 1/4 cup unsweetened cocoa powder

DIRECTIONS

1. Preheat oven to 375 degrees F (190 degrees C). Grease 3 9-inch cake pans.
2. Beat whites of 4 eggs in a glass or metal bowl until foamy. Continue to beat until stiff peaks form. Lift your beater or whisk straight up: the tip of the peak formed by the egg whites should curl over

slightly. Set aside. Reserve egg yolks in a small bowl. Sift together cake flour and baking powder in a separate bowl.

3. Beat 3/4 cup butter, 2 cups sugar, and 1/2 teaspoon salt with an electric mixer in a large bowl until light and fluffy. The mixture should be noticeably lighter in color. Add reserved egg yolks one at a time, allowing each yolk to blend into the butter mixture before adding the next. Pour in cake flour mixture alternately with 1 cup milk, mixing until just incorporated. Stir lemon juice and 1 teaspoon vanilla extract into batter.
4. Whisk beaten egg whites a few times; use a whisk or rubber spatula to fold 1/3 of the egg white mixture into the batter to lighten it. Fold in remaining egg whites, mixing just until combined. Pour batter into prepared pans and spread evenly over bottom.
5. Bake in preheated oven until cake is light golden brown and just pulling from the sides of the pan, 15 to 20 minutes. Do not overbake. Cool in pans for 5 minutes, then invert onto cooling racks to cool completely.
6. To make custard: combine 1 1/2 cups sugar, 1/2 teaspoon salt, 1/4 cup flour, cornstarch, and 1/4 cup cocoa powder in a saucepan and mix well. In a separate bowl, whisk remaining 1/2 cup sugar into 4 beaten eggs. Pour 4 cups whole milk into saucepan and cook over medium heat, stirring constantly, until mixture begins to boil. Remove from heat and gradually pour hot milk mixture into egg mixture, whisking constantly. Add chopped chocolate and stir until chocolate melts.
7. Return custard to saucepan and cook, stirring constantly, over medium heat until mixture has thickened, about 5 minutes. Remove from heat; stir in 1 tablespoon butter and 1 tablespoon vanilla extract. Transfer custard to a bowl and allow to cool.
8. To make buttercream: place 1 cup softened butter in a mixing bowl. Gradually beat in 3 cups sifted confectioners' sugar. Beat in 1 cup sifted cocoa powder. Mix in 1 teaspoon vanilla extract to make a smooth frosting. If the frosting is too stiff, add a tablespoon of hot water or as needed, drizzling it very slowly, and mix well until desired consistency is reached.
9. To make ganache: place chocolate chips in a large mixing bowl. Heat heavy cream in a saucepan until very hot but not boiling. Remove from heat and pour over the chocolate chips. Let stand for 3 minutes, then whisk, scraping sides and bottom of the bowl, until smooth. Stir in 2 teaspoons vanilla extract. Allow to cool to room temperature, cover, and set aside. Ganache should be spreadable and not firm.
10. To assemble cake: using a long serrated knife and a gentle sawing motion, slice each cake layer in half horizontally. Cover cake plate with strips of parchment paper or foil for easier clean up. Put a dab of buttercream in the center of the plate to keep cake from shifting. Set a cake half on the plate.
11. Spread custard filling onto cake layer, taking care not to spread it too close to the edge (weight of the cake layers will cause it to spread out). Gently lay another cake round on top of the first and repeat with another custard layer. Repeat with remaining layers and custard, topping custard with the last cake layer. Chill cake for 30 minutes to allow it to firm up.
12. Frost top and sides of cake with chocolate buttercream. Chill for 30 minutes, to firm and set.
13. Spread frosted cake with ganache. Remove parchment strips or aluminum foil from cake plate. Store cake in the refrigerator.

NO-BAKE GREEK YOGURT CHEESECAKE

Servings: 10 | Prep: 20m | Cooks: 15m | Total: 3h40m | Additional: 3h5m

NUTRITION FACTS

Calories: 478 | Carbohydrates: 27g | Fat: 38.2g | Protein: 9.3g | Cholesterol: 107mg

INGREDIENTS

- 1/2 cup butter
- 1 tablespoon lemon juice
- 9 whole graham crackers
- 1 teaspoon lemon zest
- 1/4 cup packed dark brown sugar
- 1 pinch sea salt
- 1/2 teaspoon sea salt
- 1 teaspoon vanilla extract
- 2 1/2 teaspoons unflavored gelatin
- 4 cups fresh blueberries
- 1 tablespoon cold water
- 3 tablespoons packed dark brown sugar
- 3 (8 ounce) packages cream cheese, at room temperature
- 2 tablespoons poppy seeds (optional)
- 2 cups whole-milk Greek yogurt, at room temperature
- 2 tablespoons lemon juice
- 1/2 pinch white sugar
- 1 teaspoon lemon zest

DIRECTIONS

1. Heat butter in a small saucepan over medium-low heat until it smells nutty and brown bits form on the bottom, 15 to 17 minutes. Don't crank up the heat to try to get there faster; you'll just end up with burned butter.
2. Meanwhile, pulse together graham crackers, brown sugar, and salt in a food processor until fine crumbs form. Carefully pour butter into crumb mixture while food processor is running. Press combined mixture into bottom and sides of a 10-inch tart pan with a removable bottom. Chill for 1 hour or freeze for 20 minutes until set.
3. Stir together gelatin and cold water in a small bowl. Let stand for 5 minutes, then microwave until gelatin dissolves, about 10 seconds.
4. Beat cream cheese in a bowl with an electric mixer for 30 seconds. Add yogurt, white sugar, lemon juice, lemon zest, salt, and vanilla. Beat until smooth, then beat in gelatin. Pour mixture into the chilled crust. Chill until set, about 2 hours.
5. Stir together blueberries, brown sugar, poppy seeds, lemon juice, and lemon zest. Scatter topping over cheesecake.

THE REAL RED VELVET CAKE

Servings: 16 | Prep: 50m | Cooks: 30m | Total: 3h25m | Additional: 2h5m

NUTRITION FACTS

Calories: 669 | Carbohydrates: 89.1g | Fat: 33.8g | Protein: 5.9g | Cholesterol: 117mg

INGREDIENTS

- cooking spray
- 1 1/2 sticks unsalted butter, softened
- 1 1/2 cups all-purpose flour
- 3 eggs, at room temperature
- 1 1/2 cups cake flour
- 1 cup white sugar
- 1/2 cup cocoa powder
- 1 cup whole milk
- 1 1/2 teaspoons baking soda
- 1/2 cup all-purpose flour, sifted
- 1/2 teaspoon kosher salt
- 1/2 teaspoon salt
- 1 1/2 cups buttermilk
- 2 cups unsalted butter, softened
- 2 teaspoons vanilla extract
- 1 1/2 teaspoons vanilla extract
- 3 3/4 cups brown sugar

DIRECTIONS

1. Preheat the oven to 325 degrees F (163 degrees C). Line the bottoms of three 9-inch cake pans with parchment paper. Spray the sides with cooking spray.
2. Sift all-purpose flour, cake flour, cocoa powder, baking soda, and salt together in a medium bowl.
3. Microwave buttermilk just until warm, about 30 seconds. Stir in vanilla extract.
4. Beat brown sugar and butter together in a bowl until light and fluffy, about 5 minutes. Add eggs one at a time, mixing thoroughly before each addition. Blend in the flour mixture and buttermilk in 3 additions until fully combined. Let mixer run on low for 5 minutes. Distribute the cake batter between the prepared cake pans.
5. Bake in the preheated oven until a toothpick inserted into the center the cakes comes out clean, 30 to 35 minutes.
6. Let cool for 15 minutes in the pans. Turn cakes out and let cool completely on a wire rack, at least 30 minutes. Cover with plastic wrap and chill for at least 1 hour or overnight.
7. Meanwhile, whisk sugar, milk, flour, and salt together in a medium saucepan for the frosting. Cook over medium heat, whisking constantly, until the mixture thickens and begins to simmer, about 10 minutes. Pour into a medium bowl and chill for about 45 minutes, stirring occasionally.

8. Beat butter until smooth, about 5 minutes. Slowly add the milk and flour mixture, 1/4 cup at a time, beating in between each addition and scraping the sides of the bowl occasionally. Mix in the vanilla extract.
9. Level the cake layers before assembling the cake. Scoop about 2/3 cup of frosting onto the first layer and spread into an even layer. Repeat with the second and third cake layers. Frost the outsides of the cake with thin layer of frosting to catch any crumbs and chill for 20 minutes.
10. Finish frosting the cake with remaining frosting. Cut and serve.

CHANTAL'S NEW YORK CHEESECAKE

Servings: 12 | Prep: 30m | Cooks: 1h | Total: 7h30m | Additional: 6h

NUTRITION FACTS

Calories: 533 | Carbohydrates: 44.2g | Fat: 35.7g | Protein: 10.3g | Cholesterol: 159mg

INGREDIENTS

- 15 graham crackers, crushed
- 4 eggs
- 2 tablespoons butter, melted
- 1 cup sour cream
- 4 (8 ounce) packages cream cheese
- 1 tablespoon vanilla extract
- 1 1/2 cups white sugar
- 1/4 cup all-purpose flour
- 3/4 cup milk

DIRECTIONS

1. Preheat oven to 350 degrees F (175 degrees C). Grease a 9 inch springform pan.
2. In a medium bowl, mix graham cracker crumbs with melted butter. Press onto bottom of springform pan.
3. In a large bowl, mix cream cheese with sugar until smooth. Blend in milk, and then mix in the eggs one at a time, mixing just enough to incorporate. Mix in sour cream, vanilla and flour until smooth. Pour filling into prepared crust.
4. Bake in preheated oven for 1 hour. Turn the oven off, and let cake cool in oven with the door closed for 5 to 6 hours; this prevents cracking. Chill in refrigerator until serving.

CARROT CAKE

Servings: 18 | Prep: 30m | Cooks: 1h | Total: 2h | Additional: 30m

NUTRITION FACTS

Calories: 575 | Carbohydrates: 63.7g | Fat: 34.8g | Protein: 5.1g | Cholesterol: 69mg

INGREDIENTS

- 4 eggs
- 2 teaspoons ground cinnamon
- 1 1/4 cups vegetable oil
- 3 cups grated carrots
- 2 cups white sugar
- 1 cup chopped pecans
- 2 teaspoons vanilla extract
- 1/2 cup butter, softened
- 2 cups all-purpose flour
- 8 ounces cream cheese, softened
- 2 teaspoons baking soda
- 4 cups confectioners' sugar
- 2 teaspoons baking powder
- 1 teaspoon vanilla extract
- 1/2 teaspoon salt
- 1 cup chopped pecans

DIRECTIONS

1. Preheat oven to 350 degrees F (175 degrees C). Grease and flour a 9x13 inch pan.
2. In a large bowl, beat together eggs, oil, white sugar and 2 teaspoons vanilla. Mix in flour, baking soda, baking powder, salt and cinnamon. Stir in carrots. Fold in pecans. Pour into prepared pan.
3. Bake in the preheated oven for 40 to 50 minutes, or until a toothpick inserted into the center of the cake comes out clean. Let cool in pan for 10 minutes, then turn out onto a wire rack and cool completely.
4. To Make Frosting: In a medium bowl, combine butter, cream cheese, confectioners' sugar and 1 teaspoon vanilla. Beat until the mixture is smooth and creamy. Stir in chopped pecans. Frost the cooled cake.

DOUBLE LAYER PUMPKIN CHEESECAKE

Servings: 8 | Prep: 30m | Cooks: 40m | Total: 4h10m | Additional: 3h

NUTRITION FACTS

Calories: 426 | Carbohydrates: 35.5g | Fat: 29g | Protein: 7.2g | Cholesterol: 108mg

INGREDIENTS

- 2 (8 ounce) packages cream cheese, softened
- 1/2 cup pumpkin puree

- 1/2 cup white sugar
- 1/2 teaspoon ground cinnamon
- 1/2 teaspoon vanilla extract
- 1 pinch ground cloves
- 2 eggs
- 1 pinch ground nutmeg
- 1 (9 inch) prepared graham cracker crust
- 1/2 cup frozen whipped topping, thawed

DIRECTIONS

1. Preheat oven to 325 degrees F (165 degrees C).
2. In a large bowl, combine cream cheese, sugar and vanilla. Beat until smooth. Blend in eggs one at a time. Remove 1 cup of batter and spread into bottom of crust; set aside.
3. Add pumpkin, cinnamon, cloves and nutmeg to the remaining batter and stir gently until well blended. Carefully spread over the batter in the crust.
4. Bake in preheated oven for 35 to 40 minutes, or until center is almost set. Allow to cool, then refrigerate for 3 hours or overnight. Cover with whipped topping before serving.

SIMPLE WHITE CAKE

Servings: 12 | Prep: 20m | Cooks: 30m | Total: 50m

NUTRITION FACTS

Calories: 209 | Carbohydrates: 29.4g | Fat: 8.9g | Protein: 3.1g | Cholesterol: 52mg

INGREDIENTS

- 1 cup white sugar
- 1 1/2 cups all-purpose flour
- 1/2 cup butter
- 1 3/4 teaspoons baking powder
- 2 eggs
- 1/2 cup milk
- 2 teaspoons vanilla extract

DIRECTIONS

1. Preheat oven to 350 degrees F (175 degrees C). Grease and flour a 9x9 inch pan or line a muffin pan with paper liners.
2. In a medium bowl, cream together the sugar and butter. Beat in the eggs, one at a time, then stir in the vanilla. Combine flour and baking powder, add to the creamed mixture and mix well. Finally stir in the milk until batter is smooth. Pour or spoon batter into the prepared pan.

3. Bake for 30 to 40 minutes in the preheated oven. For cupcakes, bake 20 to 25 minutes. Cake is done when it springs back to the touch.

ONE BOWL CHOCOLATE CAKE
Servings: 26 | Prep: 20m | Cooks: 30m | Total: 1h | Additional: 10m

NUTRITION FACTS

Calories: 157 | Carbohydrates: 25.7g | Fat: 5.7g | Protein: 2.3g | Cholesterol: 16mg

INGREDIENTS

- 2 cups white sugar
- 2 eggs
- 1 3/4 cups all-purpose flour
- 1 cup milk
- 3/4 cup unsweetened cocoa powder
- 1/2 cup vegetable oil
- 1 1/2 teaspoons baking powder
- 2 teaspoons vanilla extract
- 1 1/2 teaspoons baking soda
- 1 cup boiling water
- 1 teaspoon salt

DIRECTIONS

1. Preheat oven to 350 degrees F (175 degrees C). Grease and flour two nine inch round pans.
2. In a large bowl, stir together the sugar, flour, cocoa, baking powder, baking soda and salt. Add the eggs, milk, oil and vanilla, mix for 2 minutes on medium speed of mixer. Stir in the boiling water last. Batter will be thin. Pour evenly into the prepared pans.
3. Bake 30 to 35 minutes in the preheated oven, until the cake tests done with a toothpick. Cool in the pans for 10 minutes, then remove to a wire rack to cool completely.

WHITE CHOCOLATE RASPBERRY CHEESECAKE
Servings: 16 | Prep: 1h | Cooks: 1h | Total: 10h | Additional: 8h

NUTRITION FACTS

Calories: 412 | Carbohydrates: 34.4g | Fat: 28.3g | Protein: 6.8g | Cholesterol: 96mg

INGREDIENTS

- 1 cup chocolate cookie crumbs

- 2 cups white chocolate chips
- 3 tablespoons white sugar
- 1/2 cup half-and-half cream
- 1/4 cup butter, melted
- 3 (8 ounce) packages cream cheese, softened
- 1 (10 ounce) package frozen raspberries
- 1/2 cup white sugar
- 2 tablespoons white sugar
- 3 eggs
- 2 teaspoons cornstarch
- 1 teaspoon vanilla extract
- 1/2 cup water

DIRECTIONS

1. In a medium bowl, mix together cookie crumbs, 3 tablespoons sugar, and melted butter. Press mixture into the bottom of a 9 inch springform pan.
2. In a saucepan, combine raspberries, 2 tablespoons sugar, cornstarch, and water. Bring to boil, and continue boiling 5 minutes, or until sauce is thick. Strain sauce through a mesh strainer to remove seeds.
3. Preheat oven to 325 degrees F (165 degrees C). In a metal bowl over a pan of simmering water, melt white chocolate chips with half-and-half, stirring occasionally until smooth.
4. In a large bowl, mix together cream cheese and 1/2 cup sugar until smooth. Beat in eggs one at a time. Blend in vanilla and melted white chocolate. Pour half of batter over crust. Spoon 3 tablespoons raspberry sauce over batter. Pour remaining cheesecake batter into pan, and again spoon 3 tablespoons raspberry sauce over the top. Swirl batter with the tip of a knife to create a marbled effect.
5. Bake for 55 to 60 minutes, or until filling is set. Cool, cover with plastic wrap, and refrigerate for 8 hours before removing from pan. Serve with remaining raspberry sauce.

SAM'S FAMOUS CARROT CAKE

Servings: 15 | Prep: 20m | Cooks: 1h | Total: 1h40m | Additional: 20m

NUTRITION FACTS

Calories: 374 | Carbohydrates: 48.7g | Fat: 18.8g | Protein: 5.2g | Cholesterol: 38mg

INGREDIENTS

- 3 eggs
- 2 cups all-purpose flour
- 3/4 cup buttermilk
- 2 teaspoons baking soda

- 3/4 cup vegetable oil
- 2 cups shredded carrots
- 1 1/2 cups white sugar
- 1 cup flaked coconut
- 2 teaspoons vanilla extract
- 1 cup chopped walnuts
- 2 teaspoons ground cinnamon
- 1 (8 ounce) can crushed pineapple with juice
- 1/4 teaspoon salt
- 1 cup raisins

DIRECTIONS

1. Preheat oven to 350 degrees F (175 degrees C). Grease and flour an 8x12 inch pan.
2. In a medium bowl, sift together flour, baking soda, salt and cinnamon. Set aside.
3. In a large bowl, combine eggs, buttermilk, oil, sugar and vanilla. Mix well. Add flour mixture and mix well.
4. In a medium bowl, combine shredded carrots, coconut, walnuts, pineapple and raisins.
5. Using a large wooden spoon or a very heavy whisk, add carrot mixture to batter and fold in well.
6. Pour into prepared 8x12 inch pan, and bake at 350 degrees F (175 degrees C) for 1 hour. Check with toothpick.
7. Allow to cool for at least 20 minutes before serving.

EXTREME CHOCOLATE CAKE

Servings: 12 | Prep: 30m | Cooks: 35m | Total: 1h5m

NUTRITION FACTS

Calories: 655 | Carbohydrates: 111.1g | Fat: 24.6g | Protein: 7.3g | Cholesterol: 64mg

INGREDIENTS

- 2 cups white sugar
- 1/2 cup vegetable oil
- 1 3/4 cups all-purpose flour
- 2 teaspoons vanilla extract
- 3/4 cup unsweetened cocoa powder
- 1 cup boiling water
- 1 1/2 teaspoons baking soda
- 3/4 cup butter
- 1 1/2 teaspoons baking powder
- 1 1/2 cups unsweetened cocoa powder
- 1 teaspoon salt

- 5 1/3 cups confectioners' sugar
- 2 eggs
- 2/3 cup milk
- 1 cup milk

DIRECTIONS

1. Preheat oven to 350 degrees F (175 degrees C). Grease and flour two 9 inch cake pans.
2. Use the first set of ingredients to make the cake. In a medium bowl, stir together the sugar, flour, cocoa, baking soda, baking powder and salt. Add the eggs, milk, oil and vanilla, mix for 3 minutes with an electric mixer. Stir in the boiling water by hand. Pour evenly into the two prepared pans.
3. Bake for 30 to 35 minutes in the preheated oven, until a toothpick inserted comes out clean. Cool for 10 minutes before removing from pans to cool completely.
4. To make the frosting, use the second set of ingredients. Cream butter until light and fluffy. Stir in the cocoa and confectioners' sugar alternately with the milk and vanilla. Beat to a spreading consistency.
5. Split the layers of cooled cake horizontally, cover the top of each layer with frosting, then stack them onto a serving plate. Frost the outside of the cake.

BLACK MAGIC CAKE

Servings: 24 | Prep: 15m | Cooks: 35m | Total: 1h | Additional: 10m

NUTRITION FACTS

Calories: 155 | Carbohydrates: 25.7g | Fat: 5.5g | Protein: 2.3g | Cholesterol: 16mg

INGREDIENTS

- 1 3/4 cups all-purpose flour
- 2 eggs
- 2 cups white sugar
- 1 cup strong brewed coffee
- 3/4 cup unsweetened cocoa powder
- 1 cup buttermilk
- 2 teaspoons baking soda
- 1/2 cup vegetable oil
- 1 teaspoon baking powder
- 1 teaspoon vanilla extract
- 1 teaspoon salt

DIRECTIONS

1. Preheat oven to 350 degrees F (175 degrees C). Grease and flour two 9 inch round cake pans or one 9x13 inch pan.

2. In large bowl combine flour, sugar, cocoa, baking soda, baking powder and salt. Make a well in the center.
3. Add eggs, coffee, buttermilk, oil and vanilla. Beat for 2 minutes on medium speed. Batter will be thin. Pour into prepared pans.
4. Bake at 350 degrees F (175 degrees C) for 30 to 40 minutes, or until toothpick inserted into center of cake comes out clean. Cool for 10 minutes, then remove from pans and finish cooling on a wire rack. Fill and frost as desired.
5. Reynolds Aluminum foil can be used to keep food moist, cook it evenly, and make clean-up easier.

BANANA CAKE

Servings: 18 | Prep: 30m | Cooks: 1h | Total: 2h30m | Additional: 1h

NUTRITION FACTS

Calories: 453 | Carbohydrates: 68.6 | Fat: 18.4g | Protein: 5.2g | Cholesterol: 79mg

INGREDIENTS

- 3/4 cup butter
- 1 1/2 cups buttermilk
- 2 1/8 cups white sugar
- 2 teaspoons lemon juice
- 3 eggs
- 1 1/2 cups mashed bananas
- 2 teaspoons vanilla extract
- 1/2 cup butter, softened
- 3 cups all-purpose flour
- 1 (8 ounce) package cream cheese, softened
- 1 1/2 teaspoons baking soda
- 3 1/2 cups confectioners' sugar
- 1/4 teaspoon salt
- 1 teaspoon vanilla extract

DIRECTIONS

1. Preheat oven to 275 degrees F (135 degrees C). Grease and flour a 9x13 inch pan. In a small bowl, mix mashed bananas with lemon juice, set aside. In a medium bowl, mix flour, baking soda and salt. Set aside.
2. In a large bowl, cream 3/4 cup butter and 2 1/8 cups sugar until light and fluffy. Beat in the eggs one at a time, then stir in 2 teaspoons vanilla. Beat in the flour mixture alternately with the buttermilk. Stir in banana mixture. Pour batter into prepared pan.

3. Bake in preheated oven for 1 hour, or until a toothpick inserted into the center of the cake comes out clean. Remove from oven and place directly into freezer for 45 minutes. This will make the cake very moist.
4. For the frosting: In a large bowl, cream 1/2 cup butter and cream cheese until smooth. Beat in 1 teaspoon vanilla. Add confectioners sugar and beat on low speed until combined, then on high until frosting is smooth. Spread on cooled cake.

SOPAPILLA CHEESECAKE PIE

Servings: 12 | Prep: 15m | Cooks: 45m | Total: 3h | Additional: 2h

NUTRITION FACTS

Calories: 481 | Carbohydrates: 50.8g | Fat: 28.7g | Protein: 5.6g | Cholesterol: 61mg

INGREDIENTS

- 2 (8 ounce) packages cream cheese, softened
- 1 teaspoon ground cinnamon
- 1 3/4 cups white sugar, divided
- 1/2 cup butter, room temperature
- 1 teaspoon Mexican vanilla extract
- 1/4 cup honey
- 2 (8 ounce) cans refrigerated crescent rolls

DIRECTIONS

1. Preheat an oven to 350 degrees F (175 degrees C). Prepare a 9x13 inch baking dish with cooking spray.
2. Beat the cream cheese with 1 cup of sugar and the vanilla extract in a bowl until smooth.
3. Unroll the cans of crescent roll dough, and use a rolling pin to shape each piece into 9x13 inch rectangles. Press one piece into the bottom of a 9x13 inch baking dish. Evenly spread the cream cheese mixture into the baking dish, then cover with the remaining piece of crescent dough. Stir together 3/4 cup of sugar, cinnamon, and butter. Dot the mixture over the top of the cheesecake.
4. Bake in the preheated oven until the crescent dough has puffed and turned golden brown, about 30 minutes. Remove from the oven and drizzle with honey. Cool completely in the pan before cutting into 12 squares.

CAKE BALLS

Servings: 36 | Prep: 40m | Cooks: 30m | Total: 3h10m | Additional: 2h

NUTRITION FACTS

Calories: 124 | Carbohydrates: 19.7g | Fat: 5.2g | Protein: 1.1g | Cholesterol: 0mg

INGREDIENTS

- 1 (18.25 ounce) package chocolate cake mix
- 1 (3 ounce) bar chocolate flavored confectioners coating
- 1 (16 ounce) container prepared chocolate frosting

DIRECTIONS

1. Prepare the cake mix according to package directions using any of the recommended pan sizes. When cake is done, crumble while warm into a large bowl, and stir in the frosting until well blended.
2. Melt chocolate coating in a glass bowl in the microwave, or in a metal bowl over a pan of simmering water, stirring occasionally until smooth.
3. Use a melon baller or small scoop to form balls of the chocolate cake mixture. Dip the balls in chocolate using a toothpick or fork to hold them. Place on waxed paper to set.

TIRAMISU LAYER CAKE

Servings: 12 | Prep: 5m | Cooks: 20m | Total: 2h | Additional: 1h35m

NUTRITION FACTS

Calories: 465 | Carbohydrates: 46.3g | Fat: 28.9g | Protein: 4.4g | Cholesterol: 78mg

INGREDIENTS

- 1 (18.25 ounce) package moist white cake mix
- 2 tablespoons coffee flavored liqueur
- 1 teaspoon instant coffee powder
- 2 cups heavy cream
- 1/4 cup coffee
- 1/4 cup confectioners' sugar
- 1 tablespoon coffee flavored liqueur
- 2 tablespoons coffee flavored liqueur
- 1 (8 ounce) container mascarpone cheese
- 2 tablespoons unsweetened cocoa powder
- 1/2 cup confectioners' sugar
- 1 (1 ounce) square semisweet chocolate

DIRECTIONS

1. Preheat oven to 350 degrees F (175 degrees C). Grease and flour 3 (9 inch) pans.
2. Prepare the cake mix according to package directions. Divide two thirds of batter between 2 pans. Stir instant coffee into remaining batter; pour into remaining pan.

3. Bake in the preheated oven for 20 to 25 minutes, or until a toothpick inserted into the center of the cake comes out clean. Let cool in pan for 10 minutes, then turn out onto a wire rack and cool completely. In a measuring cup, combine brewed coffee and 1 tablespoon coffee liqueur; set aside.
4. To make the filling: In a small bowl, using an electric mixer set on low speed, combine mascarpone, 1/2 cup confectioners' sugar and 2 tablespoons coffee liqueur; beat just until smooth. Cover with plastic wrap and refrigerate.
5. To make the frosting: In a medium bowl, using an electric mixer set on medium-high speed, beat the cream, 1/4 cup confectioners' sugar and 2 tablespoons coffee liqueur until stiff. Fold 1/2 cup of cream mixture into filling mixture.
6. To assemble the cake: Place one plain cake layer on a serving plate. Using a thin skewer, poke holes in cake, about 1 inch apart. Pour one third of reserved coffee mixture over cake, then spread with half of the filling mixture. Top with coffee-flavored cake layer; poke holes in cake. Pour another third of the coffee mixture over the second layer and spread with the remaining filling. Top with remaining cake layer; poke holes in cake. Pour remaining coffee mixture on top. Spread sides and top of cake with frosting. Place cocoa in a sieve and lightly dust top of cake. Garnish with chocolate curls. Refrigerate at least 30 minutes before serving.
7. To make the chocolate curls, use a vegetable peeler and run it down the edge of the chocolate bar.

GOLDEN RUM CAKE

Servings: 12 | Prep: 30m | Cooks: 1h | Total: 1h30m

NUTRITION FACTS

Calories: 562 | Carbohydrates: 59.2g | Fat: 29.9g | Protein: 5.6g | Cholesterol: 83mg

INGREDIENTS

- 1 cup chopped walnuts
- 1/2 cup dark rum
- 1 (18.25 ounce) package yellow cake mix
- 1/2 cup butter
- 1 (3.4 ounce) package instant vanilla pudding mix
- 1/4 cup water
- 4 eggs
- 1 cup white sugar
- 1/2 cup water
- 1/2 cup dark rum
- 1/2 cup vegetable oil

DIRECTIONS

1. Preheat oven to 325 degrees F (165 degrees C). Grease and flour a 10 inch Bundt pan. Sprinkle chopped nuts evenly over the bottom of the pan.

2. In a large bowl, combine cake mix and pudding mix. Mix in the eggs, 1/2 cup water, oil and 1/2 cup rum. Blend well. Pour batter over chopped nuts in the pan.
3. Bake in the preheated oven for 60 minutes, or until a toothpick inserted into the cake comes out clean. Let sit for 10 minutes in the pan, then turn out onto serving plate. Brush glaze over top and sides. Allow cake to absorb glaze and repeat until all glaze is used.
4. To make the glaze: in a saucepan, combine butter, 1/4 cup water and 1 cup sugar. Bring to a boil over medium heat and continue to boil for 5 minutes, stirring constantly. Remove from heat and stir in 1/2 cup rum.

BEST CARROT CAKE EVER
Servings: 16 | Prep: 1h30m | Cooks: 1h | Total: 2h30m

NUTRITION FACTS

Calories: 457 | Carbohydrates: 66.3g | Fat: 20.2g | Protein: 5.9g | Cholesterol: 47mg

INGREDIENTS

- 6 cups grated carrots
- 1 cup crushed pineapple, drained
- 1 cup brown sugar
- 3 cups all-purpose flour
- 1 cup raisins
- 1 1/2 teaspoons baking soda
- 4 eggs
- 1 teaspoon salt
- 1 1/2 cups white sugar
- 4 teaspoons ground cinnamon
- 1 cup vegetable oil
- 1 cup chopped walnuts
- 2 teaspoons vanilla extract

DIRECTIONS

1. In a medium bowl, combine grated carrots and brown sugar. Set aside for 60 minutes, then stir in raisins.
2. Preheat oven to 350 degrees F (175 degrees C). Grease and flour two 10 inch cake pans.
3. In a large bowl, beat eggs until light. Gradually beat in the white sugar, oil and vanilla. Stir in the pineapple. Combine the flour, baking soda, salt and cinnamon, stir into the wet mixture until absorbed. Finally stir in the carrot mixture and the walnuts. Pour evenly into the prepared pans.
4. Bake for 45 to 50 minutes in the preheated oven, until cake tests done with a toothpick. Cool for 10 minutes before removing from pan. When completely cooled, frost with cream cheese frosting.

DAVID'S YELLOW CAKE

Servings: 12 | Prep: 20m | Cooks: 30m | Total: 50m

NUTRITION FACTS

Calories: 360 | Carbohydrates: 44.2g | Fat: 18.8g | Protein: 4.3g | Cholesterol: 178mg

INGREDIENTS

- 1 cup butter
- 1 1/2 teaspoons vanilla extract
- 1 1/2 cups white sugar
- 2 cups cake flour
- 8 egg yolks
- 2 teaspoons baking powder
- 3/4 cup milk
- 1/2 teaspoon salt

DIRECTIONS

1. Preheat oven to 350 degrees F (175 degrees C). Grease and flour 2 - 8 inch round pans. Sift together the flour, baking powder and salt. Set aside.
2. In a large bowl, cream together the butter and sugar until light and fluffy. Beat in the egg yolks one at a time, then stir in the vanilla. Beat in the flour mixture alternately with the milk, mixing just until incorporated. Pour batter into prepared pans.
3. Bake in the preheated oven for 25 to 30 minutes, or until tops spring back when lightly tapped. Cool 15 minutes before turning out onto cooling racks.

DARK CHOCOLATE CAKE

Servings: 12 | Prep: 30m | Cooks: 30m | Total: 1h20m | Additional: 20m

NUTRITION FACTS

Calories: 427 | Carbohydrates: 63.5g | Fat: 18.3g | Protein: 6.6g | Cholesterol: 103mg

INGREDIENTS

- 2 cups boiling water
- 1/2 teaspoon salt
- 1 cup unsweetened cocoa powder
- 1 cup butter, softened
- 2 3/4 cups all-purpose flour
- 2 1/4 cups white sugar
- 2 teaspoons baking soda

- 4 eggs
- 1/2 teaspoon baking powder
- 1 1/2 teaspoons vanilla extract

DIRECTIONS

1. Preheat oven to 350 degrees F (175 degrees C). Grease 3 - 9 inch round cake pans. In medium bowl, pour boiling water over cocoa, and whisk until smooth. Let mixture cool. Sift together flour, baking soda, baking powder and salt; set aside.
2. In a large bowl, cream butter and sugar together until light and fluffy. Beat in eggs one at time, then stir in vanilla. Add the flour mixture alternately with the cocoa mixture. Spread batter evenly between the 3 prepared pans.
3. Bake in preheated oven for 25 to 30 minutes. Allow to cool.

CHOCOLATE CAVITY MAKER CAKE

Servings: 12 | Prep: 30m | Cooks: 1h | Total: 2h | Additional: 30m

NUTRITION FACTS

Calories: 528 | Carbohydrates: 66g | Fat: 26.4g | Protein: 6.1g | Cholesterol: 63mg

INGREDIENTS

- 1 (18.25 ounce) package dark chocolate cake mix
- 1/3 cup vegetable oil
- 1 (3.9 ounce) package instant chocolate pudding mix
- 1/2 cup coffee flavored liqueur
- 1 (16 ounce) container sour cream
- 2 cups semisweet chocolate chips
- 3 eggs

DIRECTIONS

1. Preheat oven to 350 degrees F (175 degrees C). Grease and flour a 10 inch Bundt pan.
2. In a large bowl, combine cake mix, pudding mix, sour cream, eggs, oil and coffee liqueur. Beat until ingredients are well blended. Fold in chocolate chips. Batter will be thick. Spoon into prepared pan.
3. Bake in preheated oven for 1 hour, or until cake springs back when lightly tapped. Cool 10 minutes in pan, then turn out and cool completely on wire rack.

CREAM CHEESE POUND CAKE

Servings: 14 | Prep: 30m | Cooks: 1h | Total: 1h30m

NUTRITION FACTS

Calories: 525 | Carbohydrates: 63.9g | Fat: 27.7g | Protein: 6.9g | Cholesterol: 150mg

INGREDIENTS

- 1 (8 ounce) package cream cheese
- 6 eggs
- 1 1/2 cups butter
- 3 cups all-purpose flour
- 3 cups white sugar
- 1 teaspoon vanilla extract

DIRECTIONS

1. Preheat oven to 325 degrees F (160 degrees C) grease and flour a 10 inch tube pan.
2. In a large bowl, cream butter and cream cheese until smooth. Add sugar gradually and beat until fluffy.
3. Add eggs two at a time, beating well with each addition. Add the flour all at once and mix in. Add vanilla.
4. Pour into a 10 inch tube pan. Bake at 325 degrees F (160 degrees C) for 1 hour and 20 minutes. Check for doneness at 1 hour. A toothpick inserted into center of cake will come out clean.

RED VELVET CUPCAKES

Servings: 30 | Prep: 20m | Cooks: 20m | Total: 40m

NUTRITION FACTS

Calories: 276 | Carbohydrates: 37.8g | Fat: 13.1g | Protein: 3.2g | Cholesterol: 57mg

INGREDIENTS

- 2 1/2 cups flour
- 1 (1 ounce) bottle McCormick Red Food Color
- 1/2 cup unsweetened cocoa powder
- 2 teaspoons McCormick Pure Vanilla Extract
- 1 teaspoon baking soda
- 1 (8 ounce) package cream cheese, softened
- 1/2 teaspoon salt
- 1/4 cup butter, softened
- 1 cup butter, softened
- 2 tablespoons sour cream
- 2 cups sugar
- 2 teaspoons McCormick Pure Vanilla Extract
- 4 eggs

- 1 (16 ounce) box confectioners' sugar
- 1 cup sour cream
- 1/2 cup milk

DIRECTIONS

1. Preheat oven to 350 degrees F. Mix flour, cocoa powder, baking soda and salt in medium bowl. Set aside.
2. Beat butter and sugar in large bowl with electric mixer on medium speed 5 minutes or until light and fluffy. Beat in eggs, one at a time. Mix in sour cream, milk, food color and vanilla. Gradually beat in flour mixture on low speed until just blended. Do not overbeat. Spoon batter into 30 paper-lined muffin cups, filling each cup 2/3 full.
3. Bake 20 minutes or until toothpick inserted into cupcake comes out clean. Cool in pans on wire rack 5 minutes. Remove from pans; cool completely. Frost with Vanilla Cream Cheese Frosting.
4. Vanilla Cream Cheese Frosting: Beat cream cheese, softened, butter, sour cream and McCormick(R) Pure Vanilla Extract in large bowl until light and fluffy. Gradually beat in confectioners' sugar until smooth.

CHOCOLATE CUPCAKES

Servings: 16 | Prep: 15m | Cooks: 15m | Total: 30m

NUTRITION FACTS

Calories: 158 | Carbohydrates: 29.8g | Fat: 3.9g | Protein: 3.2g | Cholesterol: 30mg

INGREDIENTS

- 1 1/3 cups all-purpose flour
- 3 tablespoons butter, softened
- 1/4 teaspoon baking soda
- 1 1/2 cups white sugar
- 2 teaspoons baking powder
- 2 eggs
- 3/4 cup unsweetened cocoa powder
- 3/4 teaspoon vanilla extract
- 1/8 teaspoon salt
- 1 cup milk

DIRECTIONS

1. Preheat oven to 350 degrees F (175 degrees C). Line a muffin pan with paper or foil liners. Sift together the flour, baking powder, baking soda, cocoa and salt. Set aside.
2. In a large bowl, cream together the butter and sugar until light and fluffy. Add the eggs one at a time, beating well with each addition, then stir in the vanilla. Add the flour mixture alternately with the milk; beat well. Fill the muffin cups 3/4 full.

3. Bake for 15 to 17 minutes in the preheated oven, or until a toothpick inserted into the cake comes out clean. Frost with your favorite frosting when cool.

GRANNY KAT'S PUMPKIN ROLL

Servings: 10 | Prep: 20m | Cooks: 15m | Total: 55m | Additional: 20m

NUTRITION FACTS

Calories: 316 | Carbohydrates: 43.7g | Fat: 14.1g | Protein: 4.9g | Cholesterol: 93mg

INGREDIENTS

- 3/4 cup all-purpose flour
- 1 teaspoon lemon juice
- 1 cup white sugar
- 2 tablespoons confectioners' sugar
- 1 teaspoon baking soda
- 1 (8 ounce) package cream cheese, softened
- 2 teaspoons pumpkin pie spice
- 1/4 cup butter
- 1 cup pumpkin puree
- 1 teaspoon vanilla extract
- 3 eggs
- 1 cup confectioners' sugar

DIRECTIONS

1. Preheat oven to 375 degrees F (190 degrees C). Grease and flour a 9x13 inch jelly roll pan or cookie sheet.
2. In a large bowl, mix together flour, sugar, baking soda, and pumpkin pie spice. Stir in pumpkin puree, eggs, and lemon juice. Pour mixture into prepared pan. Spread the mixture evenly.
3. Bake at 375 degrees F (190 degrees C) for 15 minutes.
4. Lay a damp linen towel on the counter, sprinkle it with confectioner's sugar, and turn the cake onto the towel. Carefully roll the towel up (lengthwise) with the cake in it. Place the cake-in-towel on a cooling rack and let it cool for 20 minutes.
5. Make the icing: In a medium bowl, blend cream cheese, butter, vanilla, and sugar with a wooden spoon or electric mixer.
6. When the cake has cooled 20 minutes, unroll it and spread icing onto it. Immediately re-roll (not in the towel this time), and wrap it with plastic wrap. Keep the cake refrigerated or freeze it for up to 2 weeks in aluminum foil. Cut the cake in slices just before serving.

FAVORITE OLD FASHIONED GINGERBREAD

Servings: 9 | Prep: 25m | Cooks: 1h | Total: 1h45m | Additional: 20m

NUTRITION FACTS

Calories: 375 | Carbohydrates: 65.3g | Fat: 11.2g | Protein: 4.4g | Cholesterol: 48mg

INGREDIENTS

- 1/2 cup white sugar
- 1 teaspoon ground cinnamon
- 1/2 cup butter
- 1 teaspoon ground ginger
- 1 egg
- 1/2 teaspoon ground cloves
- 1 cup molasses
- 1/2 teaspoon salt
- 2 1/2 cups all-purpose flour
- 1 cup hot water
- 1 1/2 teaspoons baking soda

DIRECTIONS

1. Preheat oven to 350 degrees F (175 degrees C). Grease and flour a 9-inch square pan.
2. In a large bowl, cream together the sugar and butter. Beat in the egg, and mix in the molasses.
3. In a bowl, sift together the flour, baking soda, salt, cinnamon, ginger, and cloves. Blend into the creamed mixture. Stir in the hot water. Pour into the prepared pan.
4. Bake 1 hour in the preheated oven, until a knife inserted in the center comes out clean. Allow to cool in pan before serving.

BLUEBERRY SOUR CREAM COFFEE CAKE

Servings: 12 | Prep: 20m | Cooks: 1h | Total: 1h20m

NUTRITION FACTS

Calories: 459 | Carbohydrates: 59.5g | Fat: 24g | Protein: 4.1g | Cholesterol: 80mg

INGREDIENTS

- 1 cup butter, softened
- 1/4 teaspoon salt
- 2 cups white sugar
- 1 cup fresh or frozen blueberries
- 2 eggs

- 1/2 cup brown sugar
- 1 cup sour cream
- 1 teaspoon ground cinnamon
- 1 teaspoon vanilla extract
- 1/2 cup chopped pecans
- 1 5/8 cups all-purpose flour
- 1 tablespoon confectioners' sugar for dusting
- 1 teaspoon baking powder

DIRECTIONS

1. Preheat the oven to 350 degrees F (175 degrees C). Grease and flour a 9 inch Bundt pan.
2. In a large bowl, cream together the butter and sugar until light and fluffy. Beat in the eggs one at a time, then stir in the sour cream and vanilla. Combine the flour, baking powder, and salt; stir into the batter just until blended. Fold in blueberries.
3. Spoon half of the batter into the prepared pan. In a small bowl, stir together the brown sugar, cinnamon and pecans. Sprinkle half of this mixture over the batter in the pan. Spoon remaining batter over the top, and then sprinkle the remaining pecan mixture over. Use a knife or thin spatula to swirl the sugar layer into the cake.
4. Bake for 55 to 60 minutes in the preheated oven, or until a knife inserted into the crown of the cake comes out clean. Cool in the pan over a wire rack. Invert onto a serving plate, and tap firmly to remove from the pan. Dust with confectioners' sugar just before serving.

BETTER THAN SEX CAKE

Servings: 24 | Prep: 30m | Cooks: 1h | Total: 1h30m

NUTRITION FACTS

Calories: 193 | Carbohydrates: 29.3g | Fat: 7.6g | Protein: 2.7g | Cholesterol: 10mg

INGREDIENTS

- 1 (18.25 ounce) package devil's food cake mix
- 3 (1.4 ounce) bars chocolate covered toffee, chopped
- 1/2 (14 ounce) can sweetened condensed milk
- 1 (8 ounce) container frozen whipped topping, thawed
- 6 ounces caramel ice cream topping

DIRECTIONS

1. Bake cake according to package directions for a 9x13 inch pan; cool on wire rack for 5 minutes. Make slits across the top of the cake, making sure not to go through to the bottom.
2. In a saucepan over low heat, combine sweetened condensed milk and caramel topping, stirring until smooth and blended. Slowly pour the warm topping mixture over the top of the warm cake, letting it

sink into the slits; then sprinkle the crushed chocolate toffee bars liberally across the entire cake while still warm. (Hint: I crush my candy bars into small chunks as opposed to crumbs - I like to have pieces I can chew on!)
3. Let cake cool completely, then top with whipped topping. Decorate the top of the cake with some more chocolate toffee bar chunks and swirls of caramel topping. Refrigerate and serve right from the pan.

MICROWAVE CHOCOLATE MUG CAKE

Servings: 1 | Prep: 5m | Cooks: 2m | Total: 7m

NUTRITION FACTS

Calories: 603 | Carbohydrates: 82g | Fat: 30.4g | Protein: 6.9g | Cholesterol: 4mg

INGREDIENTS

- 1/4 cup all-purpose flour
- 3 tablespoons milk
- 1/4 cup white sugar
- 2 tablespoons canola oil
- 2 tablespoons unsweetened cocoa powder
- 1 tablespoon water
- 1/8 teaspoon baking soda
- 1/4 teaspoon vanilla extract
- 1/8 teaspoon salt

DIRECTIONS

1. Mix flour, sugar, cocoa powder, baking soda, and salt in a large microwave-safe mug; stir in milk, canola oil, water, and vanilla extract.
2. Cook in microwave until cake is done in the middle, about 1 minute 45 seconds.

KENTUCKY BUTTER CAKE

Servings: 12 | Prep: 30m | Cooks: 1h | Total: 2h | Additional: 30m

NUTRITION FACTS

Calories: 508 | Carbohydrates: 71.1g | Fat: 22.6g | Protein: 6.2g | Cholesterol: 117mg

INGREDIENTS

- 3 cups unbleached all-purpose flour
- 2 teaspoons vanilla extract

- 2 cups white sugar
- 4 eggs
- 1 teaspoon salt
- 3/4 cup white sugar
- 1 teaspoon baking powder
- 1/3 cup butter
- 1/2 teaspoon baking soda
- 3 tablespoons water
- 1 cup buttermilk
- 2 teaspoons vanilla extract
- 1 cup butter

DIRECTIONS

1. Preheat oven to 325 degrees F (165 degrees C). Grease and flour a 10 inch Bundt pan.
2. In a large bowl, mix the flour, 2 cups sugar, salt, baking powder and baking soda. Blend in buttermilk, 1 cup of butter, 2 teaspoons of vanilla and 4 eggs. Beat for 3 minutes at medium speed. Pour batter into prepared pan.
3. Bake in preheated oven for 60 minutes, or until a wooden toothpick inserted into center of cake comes out clean. Prick holes in the still warm cake. Slowly pour sauce over cake. Let cake cool before removing from pan.
4. To Make Butter Sauce: In a saucepan combine the remaining 3/4 cups sugar, 1/3 cup butter, 2 teaspoons vanilla, and the water. Cook over medium heat, until fully melted and combined, but do not boil.

IRISH CREAM BUNDT CAKE

Servings: 12 | Prep: 15m | Cooks: 1h | Total: 1h30m | Additional: 15m

NUTRITION FACTS

Calories: 590 | Carbohydrates: 68.4g | Fat: 30.1g | Protein: 4.9g | Cholesterol: 83mg

INGREDIENTS

- 1 cup chopped pecans
- 3/4 cup Irish cream liqueur
- 1 (18.25 ounce) package yellow cake mix
- 1/2 cup butter
- 1 (3.4 ounce) package instant vanilla pudding mix
- 1/4 cup water
- 4 eggs
- 1 cup white sugar
- 1/4 cup water

- 1/4 cup Irish cream liqueur
- 1/2 cup vegetable oil

DIRECTIONS

1. Preheat oven to 325 degrees F (165 degrees C). Grease and flour a 10 inch Bundt pan. Sprinkle chopped nuts evenly over bottom of pan.
2. In a large bowl, combine cake mix and pudding mix. Mix in eggs, 1/4 cup water, 1/2 cup oil and 3/4 cup Irish cream liqueur. Beat for 5 minutes at high speed. Pour batter over nuts in pan.
3. Bake in the preheated oven for 60 minutes, or until a toothpick inserted into the cake comes out clean. Cool for 10 minutes in the pan, then invert onto the serving dish. Prick top and sides of cake. Spoon glaze over top and brush onto sides of cake. Allow to absorb glaze repeat until all glaze is used up.
4. To make the glaze: In a saucepan, combine butter, 1/4 cup water and 1 cup sugar. Bring to a boil and continue boiling for 5 minutes, stirring constantly. Remove from heat and stir in 1/4 cup Irish cream.

STRAWBERRY CAKE FROM SCRATCH

Servings: 14 | Prep: 10m | Cooks: 30m | Total: 40m

NUTRITION FACTS

Calories: 393 | Carbohydrates: 59.3g | Fat: 15.4g | Protein: 5.4g | Cholesterol: 90mg

INGREDIENTS

- 2 cups white sugar
- 2 1/2 teaspoons baking powder
- 1 (3 ounce) package strawberry flavored Jell-O
- 1 cup whole milk, room temperature
- 1 cup butter, softened
- 1 tablespoon vanilla extract
- 4 eggs (room temperature)
- 1/2 cup strawberry puree made from frozen sweetened strawberries
- 2 3/4 cups sifted cake flour

DIRECTIONS

1. Preheat the oven to 350 degrees F (175 degrees C). Grease and flour two 9 inch round cake pans.
2. In a large bowl, cream together the butter, sugar and dry strawberry gelatin until light and fluffy. Beat in eggs one at a time, mixing well after each. Combine the flour and baking powder; stir into the batter alternately with the milk. Blend in vanilla and strawberry puree. Divide the batter evenly between the prepared pans.

3. Bake for 25 to 30 minutes in the preheated oven, or until a small knife inserted into the center of the cake comes out clean. Allow cakes to cool in their pans over a wire rack for at least 10 minutes, before tapping out to cool completely.

MINI CHEESECAKES

Servings: 48 | Prep: 30m | Cooks: 15m | Total: 45m

NUTRITION FACTS

Calories: 95 | Carbohydrates: 11.8g | Fat: 4.8g | Protein: 1.3g | Cholesterol: 18mg

INGREDIENTS

- 1 (12 ounce) package vanilla wafers
- 2 eggs
- 2 (8 ounce) packages cream cheese
- 1 teaspoon vanilla extract
- 3/4 cup white sugar
- 1 (21 ounce) can cherry pie filling

DIRECTIONS

1. Preheat oven to 350 degrees F (175 degrees C). Line miniature muffin tins (tassie pans) with miniature paper liners.
2. Crush the vanilla wafers, and place 1/2 teaspoon of the crushed vanilla wafers into each paper cup.
3. In a mixing bowl, beat cream cheese, sugar, eggs and vanilla until light and fluffy. Fill each miniature muffin liner with this mixture, almost to the top.
4. Bake for 15 minutes. Cool. Top with a teaspoonful of cherry pie filling.

AWESOME CARROT CAKE WITH CREAM CHEESE FROSTING

Servings: 24 | Prep: 30m | Cooks: 40m | Total: 1h40m | Additional: 30m

NUTRITION FACTS

Calories: 369 | Carbohydrates: 46.5g | Fat: 19.6g | Protein: 4g | Cholesterol: 48mg

INGREDIENTS

- 3 cups grated carrots
- 3/4 cup vegetable oil
- 2 cups all-purpose flour
- 1 1/4 teaspoons vanilla extract

- 2 cups white sugar
- 1 (8 ounce) can crushed pineapple with juice
- 2 teaspoons baking soda
- 3/4 cup chopped pecans
- 1 teaspoon baking powder
- 3 1/2 cups confectioners' sugar
- 1/2 teaspoon salt
- 1 (8 ounce) package Neufchatel cheese
- 1 teaspoon ground cinnamon
- 1/2 cup butter, softened
- 4 eggs
- 1 1/4 teaspoons vanilla extract
- 1 cup chopped pecans

DIRECTIONS

1. Preheat oven to 350 degrees F (175 degrees C). Grease and flour a 9x13 inch pan.
2. In a large bowl, combine grated carrots, flour, white sugar, baking soda, baking powder, salt and cinnamon. Stir in eggs, applesauce, oil, 1 1/4 teaspoon vanilla, pineapple and 3/4 cup chopped pecans. Spoon batter into prepared pan.
3. Bake in the preheated oven for 30 to 40 minutes, or until a toothpick inserted into the center of the cake comes out clean. Allow to cool.
4. To Make Frosting: In a medium bowl, combine confectioners' sugar, Neufchatel cheese, 1/2 cup butter or margarine and 1 1/4 teaspoons vanilla. Beat until smooth, then stir in 1 cup chopped pecans. Spread on cooled cake.

ECLAIR CAKE

Servings: 14 | Prep: 25m | Cooks: 4h | Total: 4h25m | Additional: 4h

NUTRITION FACTS

Calories: 395 | Carbohydrates: 64.6g | Fat: 14.2g | Protein: 4.5g | Cholesterol: 4mg

INGREDIENTS

- 2 (3.5 ounce) packages instant vanilla pudding mix
- 1 (16 ounce) package graham cracker squares
- 1 (8 ounce) container frozen whipped topping, thawed
- 1 (16 ounce) package prepared chocolate frosting
- 3 cups milk

DIRECTIONS

1. Stir pudding mix, whipped topping, and milk together in a medium bowl until well blended.
2. Arrange a single layer of graham cracker squares in the bottom of a 13x9 inch baking pan. Evenly spread half of the pudding mixture over the crackers. Top with another layer of crackers and the remaining pudding mixture. Top with a final layer of graham crackers.
3. Spread the frosting over the whole cake up to the edges of the pan. Cover, and chill at least 4 hours before serving.

HONEY BUN CAKE

Servings: 24 | Prep: 30m | Cooks: 1h | Total: 1h45m | Additional: 15m

NUTRITION FACTS

Calories: 251 | Carbohydrates: 33.6g | Fat: 12.3g | Protein: 2.4g | Cholesterol: 36mg

INGREDIENTS

- 1 (18.25 ounce) package yellow cake mix
- 1 tablespoon ground cinnamon
- 3/4 cup vegetable oil
- 2 cups confectioners' sugar
- 4 eggs
- 4 tablespoons milk
- 1 (8 ounce) container sour cream
- 1 tablespoon vanilla extract
- 1 cup brown sugar

DIRECTIONS

1. Preheat oven to 325 degrees F (165 degrees C).
2. In a large mixing bowl, combine cake mix, oil, eggs and sour cream. Stir by hand approximately 50 strokes, or until most large lumps are gone. Pour half of the batter into an ungreased 9x13 inch glass baking dish. Combine the brown sugar and cinnamon, and sprinkle over the batter in the cake pan. Spoon the other half of the batter into the cake pan, covering the brown sugar and cinnamon. Twirl the cake with a butter knife or icing knife until it looks like a honey bun (or whatever design you want to make).
3. Bake in preheated oven for 40 minutes, or until a toothpick inserted into the center of the cake comes out clean. Frost cake while it is still fairly hot. Serve warm.
4. To Make the frosting: In a small bowl, whisk together the confectioner's sugar, milk and vanilla until smooth.

CHOCOLATE LOVERS' FAVORITE CAKE

Servings: 12 | Prep: 30m | Cooks: 1h | Total: 2h | Additional: 30m

NUTRITION FACTS

Calories: 604 | Carbohydrates: 57.7g | Fat: 40g | Protein: 8.8g | Cholesterol: 144mg

INGREDIENTS

- 1 (18.25 ounce) package devil's food cake mix
- 5 eggs
- 1 (3.9 ounce) package instant chocolate pudding mix
- 1 teaspoon almond extract
- 2 cups sour cream
- 2 cups semisweet chocolate chips
- 1 cup melted butter

DIRECTIONS

1. Preheat oven to 350 degrees F (175 degrees C). Grease a 10 inch Bundt pan.
2. In a large bowl, stir together cake mix and pudding mix. Make a well in the center and pour in sour cream, melted butter, eggs and almond extract. Beat on low speed until blended. Scrape bowl, and beat 4 minutes on medium speed. Blend in chocolate chips. Pour batter into prepared pan.
3. Bake in preheated oven for 50 to 55 minutes. Let cool in pan for 10 minutes, then turn out onto a wire rack and cool completely.

COCONUT POKE CAKE

Servings: 24 | Prep: 30m | Cooks: 1h | Total: 2h | Additional: 30m

NUTRITION FACTS

Calories: 304 | Carbohydrates: 43.4g | Fat: 13.8g | Protein: 3g | Cholesterol: 6mg

INGREDIENTS

- 1 (18.25 ounce) package white cake mix
- 1 (16 ounce) package frozen whipped topping, thawed
- 1 (14 ounce) can cream of coconut
- 1 (8 ounce) package flaked coconut
- 1 (14 ounce) can sweetened condensed milk

DIRECTIONS

1. Prepare and bake white cake mix according to package directions. Remove cake from oven. While still hot, using a utility fork, poke holes all over the top of the cake.
2. Mix cream of coconut and sweetened condensed milk together. Pour over the top of the still hot cake. Let cake cool completely then frost with the whipped topping and top with the flaked coconut. Keep cake refrigerated.

PUMPKIN CAKE

Servings: 14 | Prep: 30m | Cooks: 30m | Total: 1h

NUTRITION FACTS

Calories: 438 | Carbohydrates: 46.8g | Fat: 26.8g | Protein: 5.3g | Cholesterol: 53mg

INGREDIENTS

- 2 cups white sugar
- 3 teaspoons baking powder
- 1 1/4 cups vegetable oil
- 2 teaspoons baking soda
- 1 teaspoon vanilla extract
- 1/4 teaspoon salt
- 2 cups canned pumpkin
- 2 teaspoons ground cinnamon
- 4 eggs
- 1 cup chopped walnuts (optional)
- 2 cups all-purpose flour

DIRECTIONS

1. Preheat oven to 350 degrees F (175 degrees C). Grease and flour a 12x18 inch pan. Sift together the flour, baking powder, baking soda, salt and cinnamon. Set aside.
2. In a large bowl combine sugar and oil. Blend in vanilla and pumpkin, then beat in eggs one at a time. Gradually beat in flour mixture. Stir in nuts. Spread batter into prepared 12x18 inch pan.
3. Bake in the preheated oven for 30 minutes, or until a toothpick inserted into the center of the cake comes out clean. Allow to cool.

PEACH COBBLER DUMP CAKE

Servings: 24 | Prep: 10m | Cooks: 45m | Total: 55m

NUTRITION FACTS

Calories: 155 | Carbohydrates: 24.3g | Fat: 6.4g | Protein: 1.2g | Cholesterol: 11mg

INGREDIENTS

- 2 (16 ounce) cans peaches in heavy syrup
- 1/2 cup butter
- 1 (18.25 ounce) package yellow cake mix
- 1/2 teaspoon ground cinnamon, or to taste

DIRECTIONS

1. Preheat oven to 375 degrees F (190 degrees C).
2. Empty peaches into the bottom of one 9x13 inch pan. Cover with the dry cake mix and press down firmly. Cut butter into small pieces and place on top of cake mix. Sprinkle top with cinnamon.
3. Bake at 375 degrees F (190 degrees C) for 45 minutes.

AUTUMN CHEESECAKE

Servings: 12 | Prep: 30m | Cooks: 1h10m | Total: 4h | Additional: 2h20m

NUTRITION FACTS

Calories: 341 | Carbohydrates: 30.3g | Fat: 23.4g | Protein: 5.1g | Cholesterol: 82mg

INGREDIENTS

- 1 cup graham cracker crumbs
- 2 eggs
- 1/2 cup finely chopped pecans
- 1/2 teaspoon vanilla extract
- 3 tablespoons white sugar
- 4 cups apples - peeled, cored and thinly sliced
- 1/2 teaspoon ground cinnamon
- 1/3 cup white sugar
- 1/4 cup unsalted butter, melted
- 1/2 teaspoon ground cinnamon
- 2 (8 ounce) packages cream cheese, softened
- 1/4 cup chopped pecans
- 1/2 cup white sugar

DIRECTIONS

1. Preheat oven to 350 degrees F (175 degrees C). In a large bowl, stir together the graham cracker crumbs, 1/2 cup finely chopped pecans, 3 tablespoons sugar, 1/2 teaspoon cinnamon and melted butter; press into the bottom of a 9 inch springform pan. Bake in preheated oven for 10 minutes.
2. In a large bowl, combine cream cheese and 1/2 cup sugar. Mix at medium speed until smooth. Beat in eggs one at a time, mixing well after each addition. Blend in vanilla; pour filling into the baked crust.
3. In a small bowl, stir together 1/3 cup sugar and 1/2 teaspoon cinnamon. Toss the cinnamon-sugar with the apples to coat. Spoon apple mixture over cream cheese layer and sprinkle with 1/4 cup chopped pecans.
4. Bake in preheated oven for 60 to 70 minutes. With a knife, loosen cake from rim of pan. Let cool, then remove the rim of pan. Chill cake before serving.

WHITE ALMOND WEDDING CAKE

Servings: 20 | Prep: 10m | Cooks: 25m | Total: 1h5m | Additional: 30m

NUTRITION FACTS

Calories: 211 | Carbohydrates: 35.3g | Fat: 6.6g | Protein: 2.9g | Cholesterol: 5mg

INGREDIENTS

- 1 (18.25 ounce) package white cake mix
- 1 cup sour cream
- 1 cup all-purpose flour
- 2 tablespoons vegetable oil
- 1 cup white sugar
- 1 teaspoon almond extract
- 3/4 teaspoon salt
- 1 teaspoon vanilla extract
- 1 1/3 cups water
- 4 egg whites

DIRECTIONS

1. Preheat oven to 325 degrees F (165 degrees C). Grease and flour an 11x13 inch cake pan.
2. Stir together the white cake mix, flour, sugar, and salt in a large bowl until well mixed. Pour in the water, sour cream, vegetable oil, almond and vanilla extracts, and egg whites, and beat with an electric mix on low until all the ingredients are mixed and moistened but some lumps still remain, 4 minutes.
3. Pour the batter into the prepared cake pan, and bake in the preheated oven until the top is a light golden brown and a toothpick inserted into the center of the cake comes out clean, about 25 minutes. Allow to cool before frosting.

HEAVENLY WHITE CAKE

Servings: 12 | Prep: 30m | Cooks: 30m | Total: 2h | Additional: 1h

NUTRITION FACTS

Calories: 336 | Carbohydrates: 52.1g | Fat: 12.2g | Protein: 4.7g | Cholesterol: 32mg

INGREDIENTS

- 2 3/4 cups sifted cake flour
- 3/4 cup butter
- 4 teaspoons baking powder
- 1 cup milk

- 3/4 teaspoon salt
- 1 teaspoon vanilla extract
- 4 egg whites
- 1 teaspoon almond extract
- 1 1/2 cups white sugar

DIRECTIONS

1. Measure sifted cake flour, baking powder, and salt; sift together three times.
2. In a mixing bowl, beat egg whites until foamy. Add 1/2 cup sugar gradually, and continue beating only until meringue will hold up in soft peaks.
3. Beat butter until smooth. Gradually add remaining 1 cup sugar, and cream together until light and fluffy. Add sifted ingredients alternately with milk a small amount at a time, beating after each addition until smooth. Mix in flavorings. Add meringue, and mix thoroughly into batter. Spread batter in a 15 x 10 x 1 inch pan which has been lined on the bottom with parchment paper.
4. Bake at 350 degrees F (175 degrees C) for 30 to 35 minutes. Cool cake in pan 10 minutes, then remove from pan and transfer to a wire rack to finish cooling. This cake may also be baked in two 9 inch round pans for 30 to 35 minutes, or in three 8 inch round pans for 25 to 30 minutes.

PUMPKIN GINGER CUPCAKES

Servings: 24 | Prep: 20m | Cooks: 20m | Total: 1h30m | Additional: 50m

NUTRITION FACTS

Calories: 211 | Carbohydrates: 31.8g | Fat: 8.7g | Protein: 2.4g | Cholesterol: 51mg

INGREDIENTS

- 2 cups all-purpose flour
- 1/3 cup finely chopped crystallized ginger
- 1 (3.4 ounce) package instant butterscotch pudding mix
- 1 cup butter, room temperature
- 2 teaspoons baking soda
- 1 cup white sugar
- 1/4 teaspoon salt
- 1 cup packed brown sugar
- 1 tablespoon ground cinnamon
- 4 eggs, room temperature
- 1/2 teaspoon ground ginger
- 1 teaspoon vanilla extract
- 1/2 teaspoon ground allspice
- 1 (15 ounce) can pumpkin puree
- 1/4 teaspoon ground cloves

DIRECTIONS

1. Preheat an oven to 350 degrees F (175 degrees C). Grease 24 muffin cups, or line with paper muffin liners. Whisk together the flour, pudding mix, baking soda, salt, cinnamon, ground ginger, allspice, cloves, and crystallized ginger in a bowl; set aside.
2. Beat the butter, white sugar, and brown sugar with an electric mixer in a large bowl until light and fluffy. The mixture should be noticeably lighter in color. Add the eggs one at a time, allowing each egg to blend into the butter mixture before adding the next. Beat in the vanilla and pumpkin puree with the last egg. Stir in the flour mixture, mixing until just incorporated. Pour the batter into the prepared muffin cups.
3. Bake in the preheated oven until golden and the tops spring back when lightly pressed, about 20 minutes. Cool in the pans for 10 minutes before removing to cool completely on a wire rack.

AUNT ANNE'S COFFEE CAKE
Servings: 15 | Prep: 20m | Cooks: 25m | Total: 45m

NUTRITION FACTS

Calories: 235 | Carbohydrates: 34.1g | Fat: 10g | Protein: 2.9g | Cholesterol: 38mg

INGREDIENTS

- 2 cups all-purpose flour
- 3/4 cup milk, or as needed
- 3/4 cup white sugar
- 1 1/2 teaspoons vanilla extract
- 2 teaspoons baking powder
- 1/4 cup all-purpose flour
- 1/2 teaspoon salt
- 2/3 cup white sugar
- 1/2 cup butter
- 1 teaspoon ground cinnamon
- 1 egg
- 1/4 cup butter

DIRECTIONS

1. Preheat oven to 350 degrees F (175 degrees C). Grease and flour a 9x13 inch pan. Make the streusel topping: In a medium bowl, combine 1/4 cup flour, 2/3 cup sugar and 1 teaspoon cinnamon. Cut in 1/4 cup butter until mixture resembles coarse crumbs. Set aside.

2. In a large bowl, combine 2 cups flour, 3/4 cup sugar, baking powder and salt. Cut in 1/2 cup butter until mixture resembles coarse crumbs. Crack an egg into a measuring cup and then fill add milk to make 1 cup. Stir in vanilla. Pour into crumb mixture and mix just until moistened. Spread into prepared pan. Sprinkle top with streusel.
3. Bake in the preheated oven for 25 to 30 minutes, or until a toothpick inserted into the center of the cake comes out clean. Allow to cool.

CHOCOLATE ZUCCHINI CAKE

Servings: 24 | Prep: 15m | Cooks: 50m | Total: 1h5m

NUTRITION FACTS

Calories: 269 | Carbohydrates: 27.2g | Fat: 17.5g | Protein: 3.4g | Cholesterol: 31mg

INGREDIENTS

- 2 cups all-purpose flour
- 1 teaspoon ground cinnamon
- 2 cups white sugar
- 4 eggs
- 3/4 cup unsweetened cocoa powder
- 1 1/2 cups vegetable oil
- 2 teaspoons baking soda
- 3 cups grated zucchini
- 1 teaspoon baking powder
- 3/4 cup chopped walnuts
- 1/2 teaspoon salt

DIRECTIONS

1. Preheat oven to 350 degrees F (175 degrees C). Grease and flour a 9x13 inch baking pan.
2. In a medium bowl, stir together the flour, sugar, cocoa, baking soda, baking powder, salt and cinnamon. Add the eggs and oil, mix well. Fold in the nuts and zucchini until they are evenly distributed. Pour into the prepared pan.
3. Bake for 50 to 60 minutes in the preheated oven, until a knife inserted into the center comes out clean. Cool cake completely before frosting with your favorite frosting.

PINEAPPLE UPSIDE-DOWN CAKE

Servings: 12 | Prep: 20m | Cooks: 45m | Total: 1h5m

NUTRITION FACTS

Calories: 360 | Carbohydrates: 61.8g | Fat: 12.3g | Protein: 2g | Cholesterol: 20mg

INGREDIENTS

- 1/2 cup butter
- 10 maraschino cherries
- 1 1/2 cups brown sugar
- 1 (18.25 ounce) package white cake mix
- 1 (20 ounce) can sliced pineapple

DIRECTIONS

1. Melt the butter over medium high heat in the iron skillet. Remove from the heat and sprinkle the brown sugar evenly to cover the butter. Next, arrange pineapple rings around the bottom of the pan, one layer deep. Place a maraschino cherry into the center of each pineapple ring. Prepare the cake mix as directed by the manufacturer, substitute some of the pineapple juice for some of the liquid in the directions. Pour the batter over the pineapple layer.
2. Bake as directed by the cake mix directions. Cool for 10 minutes, then carefully turn out onto a plate. Do not let the cake cool too much or it will be stuck to the pan.

VEGAN CHOCOLATE CAKE

Servings: 8 | Prep: 15m | Cooks: 45m | Total: 1h

NUTRITION FACTS

Calories: 275 | Carbohydrates: 44.6g | Fat: 9.7g | Protein: 3g | Cholesterol: 0mg

INGREDIENTS

- 1 1/2 cups all-purpose flour
- 1/3 cup vegetable oil
- 1 cup white sugar
- 1 teaspoon vanilla extract
- 1/4 cup cocoa powder
- 1 teaspoon distilled white vinegar
- 1 teaspoon baking soda
- 1 cup water
- 1/2 teaspoon salt

DIRECTIONS

1. Preheat oven to 350 degrees F (175 degrees C). Lightly grease one 9x5 inch loaf pan.
2. Sift together the flour, sugar, cocoa, baking soda and salt. Add the oil, vanilla, vinegar and water. Mix together until smooth.
3. Pour into prepared pan and bake at 350 degrees F (175 degrees C) for 45 minutes. Remove from oven and allow to cool.

A-NUMBER-1 BANANA CAKE

Servings: 12 | Prep: 30m | Cooks: 30m | Total: 1h

NUTRITION FACTS

Calories: 346 | Carbohydrates: 55.8g | Fat: 12.2g | Protein: 5.5g | Cholesterol: 52mg

INGREDIENTS

- 2 1/2 cups all-purpose flour
- 3/4 cup light brown sugar
- 1 tablespoon baking soda
- 2 eggs
- 1 pinch salt
- 4 ripe bananas, mashed
- 1/2 cup unsalted butter
- 2/3 cup buttermilk
- 1 cup white sugar
- 1/2 cup chopped walnuts

DIRECTIONS

1. Preheat oven to 350 degrees F (175 degrees C). Grease and flour 2 - 8 inch round pans. In a small bowl, whisk together flour, baking soda and salt; set aside.
2. In a large bowl, cream butter, white sugar and brown sugar until light and fluffy. Beat in eggs, one at a time. Mix in the bananas. Add flour mixture alternately with the buttermilk to the creamed mixture. Stir in chopped walnuts. Pour batter into the prepared pans.
3. Bake in the preheated oven for 30 minutes. Remove from oven, and place on a damp tea towel to cool.

GARBANZO BEAN CHOCOLATE CAKE (GLUTEN FREE!)

Servings: 12 | Prep: 15m | Cooks: 40m | Total: 1h10m | Additional: 15m

NUTRITION FACTS

Calories: 229 | Carbohydrates: 36.8g | Fat: 8.5g | Protein: 5.2g | Cholesterol: 62mg

INGREDIENTS

- 1 1/2 cups semisweet chocolate chips
- 3/4 cup white sugar
- 1 (19 ounce) can garbanzo beans, rinsed and drained
- 1/2 teaspoon baking powder
- 4 eggs

- 1 tablespoon confectioners' sugar for dusting

DIRECTIONS

1. Preheat the oven to 350 degrees F (175 degrees C). Grease a 9-inch round cake pan.
2. Place the chocolate chips into a microwave-safe bowl. Cook in the microwave for about 2 minutes, stirring every 20 seconds after the first minute, until chocolate is melted and smooth. If you have a powerful microwave, reduce the power to 50 percent.
3. Combine the beans and eggs in the bowl of a food processor. Process until smooth. Add the sugar and the baking powder, and pulse to blend. Pour in the melted chocolate and blend until smooth, scraping down the corners to make sure chocolate is completely mixed. Transfer the batter to the prepared cake pan.
4. Bake for 40 minutes in the preheated oven, or until a knife inserted into the center of the cake comes out clean. Cool in the pan on a wire rack for 10 to 15 minutes before inverting onto a serving plate. Dust with confectioners' sugar just before serving.

GERMAN CHOCOLATE CAKE
Servings: 12 | Prep: 30m | Cooks: 30m | Total: 1h

NUTRITION FACTS

Calories: 735 | Carbohydrates: 88.3g | Fat: 40.6g | Protein: 9.1g | Cholesterol: 187mg

INGREDIENTS

- 1/2 cup water
- 4 egg whites
- 4 (1 ounce) squares German sweet chocolate
- 1 cup white sugar
- 1 cup butter, softened
- 1 cup evaporated milk
- 2 cups white sugar
- 1/2 cup butter
- 4 egg yolks
- 3 egg yolks, beaten
- 1 teaspoon vanilla extract
- 1 1/3 cups flaked coconut
- 1 cup buttermilk
- 1 cup chopped pecans
- 2 1/2 cups cake flour
- 1 teaspoon vanilla extract
- 1 teaspoon baking soda
- 1/2 teaspoon shortening

- 1/2 teaspoon salt
- 1 (1 ounce) square semisweet chocolate

DIRECTIONS

1. Preheat oven to 350 degrees F (175 degrees C). Grease and flour 3 - 9 inch round pans. Sift together the flour, baking soda and salt. Set aside. In a small saucepan, heat water and 4 ounces chocolate until melted. Remove from heat and allow to cool.
2. In a large bowl, cream 1 cup butter and 2 cups sugar until light and fluffy. Beat in 4 egg yolks one at a time. Blend in the melted chocolate mixture and vanilla. Beat in the flour mixture alternately with the buttermilk, mixing just until incorporated.
3. In a large glass or metal mixing bowl, beat egg whites until stiff peaks form. Fold 1/3 of the whites into the batter, then quickly fold in remaining whites until no streaks remain.
4. Pour into 3 - 9 inch pans Bake in the preheated oven for 30 minutes, or until a toothpick inserted into the center of the cake comes out clean. Allow to cool for 10 minutes in the pan, then turn out onto wire rack.
5. To make the Filling: In a saucepan combine 1 cup sugar, evaporated milk, 1/2 cup butter, and 3 egg yolks. Cook over low heat, stirring constantly until thickened. Remove from heat. Stir in coconut, pecans and vanilla. Cool until thick enough to spread.
6. Spread filling between layers and on top of cake. In a small saucepan, melt shortening and 1 ounce of chocolate. Stir until smooth and drizzle down the sides of the cake.

ORANGE CAKE

Servings: 12 | Prep: 30m | Cooks: 1h | Total: 2h | Additional: 30m

NUTRITION FACTS

Calories: 410 | Carbohydrates: 55g | Fat: 19.8g | Protein: 4.2g | Cholesterol: 73mg

INGREDIENTS

- 1 (18.25 ounce) package yellow cake mix
- 1 teaspoon lemon extract
- 1 (3 ounce) package instant lemon pudding mix
- 1/3 cup orange juice
- 3/4 cup orange juice
- 2/3 cup white sugar
- 1/2 cup vegetable oil
- 1/4 cup butter
- 4 eggs

DIRECTIONS

1. Grease a 10 inch Bundt pan. Preheat oven to 325 degrees F (165 degrees C).

2. In a large bowl, stir together cake mix and pudding mix. Make a well in the center and pour in 3/4 cup orange juice, oil, eggs and lemon extract. Beat on low speed until blended. Scrape bowl, and beat 4 minutes on medium speed. Pour batter into prepared pan.
3. Bake in preheated oven for 50 to 60 minutes. Let cool in pan for 10 minutes, then turn out onto a wire rack and cool completely.
4. In a saucepan over medium heat, cook 1/3 cup orange juice, sugar and butter for two minutes. Drizzle over cake.

MARBLED PUMPKIN CHEESECAKE

Servings: 12 | Prep: 30m | Cooks: 1h10m | Total: 7h40m | Additional: 6h

NUTRITION FACTS

Calories: 350 | Carbohydrates: 26.8g | Fat: 25.3g | Protein: 5.8g | Cholesterol: 101mg

INGREDIENTS

- 1 1/2 cups crushed gingersnap cookies
- 1 teaspoon vanilla extract
- 1/2 cup finely chopped pecans
- 3 eggs
- 1/3 cup butter, melted
- 1 cup canned pumpkin
- 2 (8 ounce) packages cream cheese, softened
- 3/4 teaspoon ground cinnamon
- 3/4 cup white sugar, divided
- 1/4 teaspoon ground nutmeg

DIRECTIONS

1. Preheat oven to 350 degrees F (175 degrees C). In a medium bowl, mix together the crushed gingersnap cookies, pecans, and butter. Press into the bottom, and about 1 inch up the sides of a 9 inch springform pan. Bake crust 10 minutes in the preheated oven. Set aside to cool.
2. In a medium bowl, mix together the cream cheese, 1/2 cup sugar, and vanilla just until smooth. Mix in eggs one at a time, blending well after each. Set aside 1 cup of the mixture. Blend 1/4 cup sugar, pumpkin, cinnamon, and nutmeg into the remaining mixture.
3. Spread the pumpkin flavored batter into the crust, and drop the plain batter by spoonfuls onto the top. Swirl with a knife to create a marbled effect.
4. Bake 55 minutes in the preheated oven, or until filling is set. Run a knife around the edge of the pan. Allow to cool before removing pan rim. Chill for at least 4 hours before serving.

BLACK BOTTOM CUPCAKES

Servings: 24 | Prep: 30m | Cooks: 30m | Total: 1hm

NUTRITION FACTS

Calories: 171 | Carbohydrates: 22.4g | Fat: 8.9g | Protein: 2.3g | Cholesterol: 18mg

INGREDIENTS

- 1 (8 ounce) package cream cheese, softened
- 1 teaspoon baking soda
- 1 egg
- 1/2 teaspoon salt
- 1/3 cup white sugar
- 1 cup water
- 1/8 teaspoon salt
- 1/3 cup vegetable oil
- 1 cup miniature semisweet chocolate chips
- 1 tablespoon cider vinegar
- 1 1/2 cups all-purpose flour
- 1 teaspoon vanilla extract
- 1 cup white sugar
- 1/4 cup unsweetened cocoa powder

DIRECTIONS

1. Preheat oven to 350 degrees F (175 degrees C). Line muffin tins with paper cups or lightly spray with non-stick cooking spray.
2. In a medium bowl, beat the cream cheese, egg, 1/3 cup sugar and 1/8 teaspoon salt until light and fluffy. Stir in the chocolate chips and set aside.
3. In a large bowl, mix together the flour, 1 cup sugar, cocoa, baking soda and 1/2 teaspoon salt. Make a well in the center and add the water, oil, vinegar and vanilla. Stir together until well blended. Fill muffin tins 1/3 full with the batter and top with a dollop of the cream cheese mixture.
4. Bake in preheated oven for 25 to 30 minutes.

FRESH STRAWBERRY UPSIDE DOWN CAKE

Servings: 12 | Prep: 15m | Cooks: 50m | Total: 1h20m | Additional: 15m

NUTRITION FACTS

Calories: 290 | Carbohydrates: 58.3g | Fat: 5g | Protein: 3.1g | Cholesterol: 1mg

INGREDIENTS

- 2 cups crushed fresh strawberries
- 3 cups miniature marshmallows
- 1 (6 ounce) package strawberry flavored Jell-O mix
- 1 (18 ounce) package yellow cake mix, batter prepared as directed on package

DIRECTIONS

1. Preheat an oven to 350 degrees F (175 degrees C).
2. Spread crushed strawberries on the bottom of a 9x13 inch baking pan. Evenly sprinkle strawberries with the dry gelatin powder, and top with mini marshmallows.
3. Prepare the cake mix as directed on the package, and pour on top of the marshmallows. Bake in the preheated oven until a toothpick inserted into the center comes out clean, about 40 to 50 minutes. Cool in the pan for 15 minutes. Run a knife around the pan to loosen the sides, and turn the cake out onto a serving tray. Store cake in the refrigerator.

STREUSEL TOPPED BLUEBERRY MUFFINS

Servings: 12 | Prep: 20m | Cooks: 25m | Total: 45m

NUTRITION FACTS

Calories: 266 | Carbohydrates: 38.9g | Fat: 10.9g | Protein: 4g | Cholesterol: 57mg

INGREDIENTS

- 2 cups all-purpose flour
- 1 teaspoon vanilla extract
- 2 teaspoons baking powder
- 1/4 teaspoon lemon zest
- 1/2 teaspoon salt
- 1/2 cup milk
- 1 1/2 tablespoons all-purpose flour
- 2 tablespoons all-purpose flour
- 1 1/2 cups fresh blueberries
- 5 tablespoons white sugar
- 1/2 cup butter
- 1/2 teaspoon ground cinnamon
- 3/4 cup white sugar
- 2 tablespoons butter, diced
- 2 eggs

DIRECTIONS

1. Preheat oven to 375 degrees F (190 degrees C). Grease 12 muffin cups or line with paper muffin liners.

2. Combine 2 cups flour, 2 teaspoons baking powder, and 1/2 teaspoon salt in medium bowl. In a small bowl, sprinkle 1 to 2 tablespoons flour over blueberries, and set aside. (This simple trick will keep you from having "purple" batter)
3. In a large bowl, beat 1/2 cup butter with 3/4 cup sugar until light and fluffy. Beat in eggs, and stir in vanilla and lemon zest. Fold in dry ingredients alternately with milk. Fold in blueberries. Remember, fold gently, don't stir. Spoon batter into prepared cups.
4. Combine 2 tablespoons flour, 5 tablespoons sugar ,and 1/2 teaspoon cinnamon in a small bowl. Cut in 2 tablespoons butter with fork or pastry blender until mixture resembles course crumbs. Sprinkle over batter in muffin cups.
5. Bake in the preheated oven for 20 to 25 minutes, or until a toothpick inserted in center of a muffin comes out clean. Cool in pans on wire rack. These muffins freeze really well, and re-heat in the microwave successfully. Hope you enjoy!!

AMAZING PECAN COFFEE CAKE

Servings: 12 | Prep: 20m | Cooks: 30m | Total: 50m

NUTRITION FACTS

Calories: 485 | Carbohydrates: 52.7g | Fat: 29.5g | Protein: 4.9g | Cholesterol: 85mg

INGREDIENTS

- 2 cups all-purpose flour
- 2 eggs
- 1/4 teaspoon salt
- 1 tablespoon vanilla extract
- 1 tablespoon baking powder
- 1/2 cup brown sugar
- 1 cup butter, softened
- 1 cup chopped pecans
- 1 cup sour cream
- 1 teaspoon ground cinnamon
- 1 1/2 cups white sugar
- 2 tablespoons butter, melted

DIRECTIONS

1. Preheat oven to 350 degrees F (175 degrees C). Line a 9x13 inch pan with aluminum foil, and lightly grease with vegetable oil or cooking spray. Sift together the flour, baking powder, and salt; set aside.
2. In a large bowl, cream the butter until light and fluffy. Gradually beat in sour cream, then beat in sugar. Beat in the eggs one at a time, then stir in the vanilla. By hand, fold in the flour mixture, mixing just until incorporated. Spread batter into prepared pan.
3. To make the Pecan Topping: In a medium bowl, mix together brown sugar, pecans and cinnamon. Stir in melted butter until crumbly. Sprinkle over cake batter in pan.
4. Bake in the preheated oven for 30 to 35 minutes, or until a toothpick inserted into the center of the cake comes out clean. Let cool in pan for 10 minutes, then turn out onto a wire rack, and remove foil.

SOUR CREAM COFFEE CAKE

Servings: 18 | Prep: 15m | Cooks: 40m | Total: 55m

NUTRITION FACTS

Calories: 306 | Carbohydrates: 41.4g | Fat: 14.9g | Protein: 2.9g | Cholesterol: 57mg

INGREDIENTS

- 1 cup butter
- 1 teaspoon baking powder
- 2 cups white sugar
- 1/8 teaspoon salt
- 2 eggs
- 1/3 cup all-purpose flour

- 1 cup sour cream
- 1/2 cup packed brown sugar
- 1/2 teaspoon vanilla extract
- 2 tablespoons melted butter
- 2 cups all-purpose flour
- 1 teaspoon ground cinnamon

DIRECTIONS

1. Preheat oven to 350 degrees F (175 degrees C). Grease a 9x13 inch baking pan.
2. In a large bowl, cream together 1 cup butter and white sugar until light and fluffy. Beat in the eggs one at a time, then stir in the sour cream and vanilla. Mix in 2 cups flour, baking powder, and salt. Spread 1/2 of batter in the prepared pan.
3. Prepare the filling: In a medium bowl mix 1/3 cup flour, brown sugar, 2 tablespoons melted butter, and cinnamon. Sprinkle cake batter with 1/2 the filling. Spread second half of batter over the filling, and top with remaining filling.
4. Bake 35 to 40 minutes in the preheated oven, or until a toothpick inserted near the center comes out clean.

CARROT CAKE

Servings: 15 | Prep: 30m | Cooks: 55m | Total: 2h | Additional: 35m

NUTRITION FACTS

Calories: 616 | Carbohydrates: 83.5g | Fat: 30.2g | Protein: 6.2g | Cholesterol: 70mg

INGREDIENTS

- 2 cups white sugar
- 2 teaspoons baking soda
- 3/4 cup vegetable oil
- 2 teaspoons ground cinnamon
- 3 eggs
- 1 1/2 teaspoons salt
- 1 teaspoon vanilla extract
- 1 cup chopped walnuts
- 3/4 cup buttermilk
- 1/2 cup butter
- 2 cups grated carrots
- 1 (8 ounce) package cream cheese
- 1 cup flaked coconut
- 1 teaspoon vanilla extract
- 1 (15 ounce) can crushed pineapple, drained

- 4 cups confectioners' sugar
- 2 cups all-purpose flour

DIRECTIONS

1. Preheat oven to 350 degrees F (175 degrees C). Grease a 9x13 inch baking pan. Set aside.
2. In a large bowl, mix together sugar, oil, eggs, vanilla, and buttermilk. Stir in carrots, coconut, vanilla, and pineapple. In a separate bowl, combine flour, baking soda, cinnamon, and salt; gently stir into carrot mixture. Stir in chopped nuts. Spread batter into prepared pan.
3. Bake for 55 minutes or until toothpick inserted into cake comes out clean. Remove from oven, and set aside to cool.
4. In a medium mixing bowl, combine butter or margarine, cream cheese, vanilla, and confectioners sugar. Blend until creamy. Frost cake while still in the pan.

TEXAS SHEET CAKE

Servings: 32 | Prep: 10m | Cooks: 20m | Total: 30m

NUTRITION FACTS

Calories: 256 | Carbohydrates: 35.8g | Fat: 12.5g | Protein: 2.4g | Cholesterol: 36mg

INGREDIENTS

- 2 cups all-purpose flour
- 1 cup water
- 2 cups white sugar
- 5 tablespoons unsweetened cocoa powder
- 1 teaspoon baking soda
- 6 tablespoons milk
- 1/2 teaspoon salt
- 5 tablespoons unsweetened cocoa powder
- 1/2 cup sour cream
- 1/2 cup butter
- 2 eggs
- 4 cups confectioners' sugar
- 1 cup butter
- 1 teaspoon vanilla extract
- 1 cup chopped walnuts (optional)

DIRECTIONS

1. Preheat oven to 350 degrees F (175 degrees C). Grease and flour a 10x15 inch pan
2. Combine the flour, sugar, baking soda and salt. Beat in the sour cream and eggs. Set aside. Melt the butter on low in a saucepan, add the water and 5 tablespoons cocoa. Bring mixture to a boil then

remove from heat. Allow to cool slightly, then stir cocoa mixture into the egg mixture, mixing until blended.
3. Pour batter into prepared pan. Bake in the preheated oven for 20 minutes, or until a toothpick inserted into the center comes out clean.
4. For the icing: In a large saucepan, combine the milk, 5 tablespoons cocoa and 1/2 cup butter. Bring to a boil, then remove from heat. Stir in the confectioners' sugar and vanilla, then fold in the nuts, mixing until blended. Spread frosting over warm cake.

CHEESECAKE SUPREME
Servings: 12 | Prep: 30m | Cooks: 1h10m | Total: 1h40m

NUTRITION FACTS

Calories: 610 | Carbohydrates: 49.4g | Fat: 42.1g | Protein: 11.1g | Cholesterol: 231mg

INGREDIENTS

- 1 1/2 cups graham cracker crumbs
- 2 egg yolks
- 1/2 cup white sugar
- 1 3/4 cups white sugar
- 1/4 cup butter, melted
- 1/8 cup all-purpose flour
- 5 (8 ounce) packages cream cheese, softened
- 1/4 cup heavy whipping cream
- 5 eggs

DIRECTIONS

1. Preheat oven to 400 degrees F (200 degrees C).
2. Mix the graham cracker crumbs, 1/2 cup of the white sugar, and the melted butter together. Press mixture into the bottom of one 9 or 10 inch springform pan.
3. In a large bowl, combine cream cheese, eggs and egg yolks; mix until smooth. Add the remaining 1 3/4 cups white sugar, the flour and the heavy cream. Blend until smooth. Pour batter into prepared pan.
4. Bake at 400 degrees F (200 degrees C) for 10 minutes, then turn oven temperature down to 200 degrees F (100 degrees C) and continue baking for 1 hour, or until filling is set. Let cheesecake cool, then refrigerate.

CAKE MIXES FROM SCRATCH AND VARIATIONS
Servings: 24 | Prep: 20m | Cooks: 35m | Total: 55m

NUTRITION FACTS

Calories: 142 | Carbohydrates: 22.5g | Fat: 5g | Protein: 2.1g | Cholesterol: 16mg

INGREDIENTS

- 2 1/3 cups all-purpose flour
- 1/2 cup shortening
- 1 tablespoon baking powder
- 2 eggs
- 3/4 teaspoon salt
- 1 cup milk
- 1 1/2 cups white sugar
- 1 teaspoon vanilla extract

DIRECTIONS

1. For a Yellow Cake: Sift together flour, baking powder, salt, and sugar. Cut in shortening until fine crumbs are formed. Add eggs, milk, and vanilla. Beat at low speed for 1 minute, then high for 2 minutes, scraping the bowl frequently.
2. Pour batter into greased and floured 9x13 inch pan. Bake in preheated 350 degree F oven (175 degrees C) for 25 to 30 minutes.
3. Variation for a White Cake: Prepare as for the basic cake except use 3 egg whites for the 2 whole eggs. Whites may be beaten separately and added for a lighter cake.
4. Variation for a Chocolate Cake: Add 1/4 cup cocoa powder to the basic cake mix prior to adding the milk.
5. Variation for a Spice Cake: Add 1 teaspoon cinnamon, 1/4 teaspoon ground cloves, and 1/4 teaspoon ground allspice to the basic cake mix.
6. Variation for a Pineapple Upside Down Cake: Melt 1/2 cup butter in the bottom of a 9x13 pan. Add 2/3 cup brown sugar, stirring into the butter. Arrange pineapple slices in the pan. Top with the basic (yellow cake) mix recipe. Bake 30 to 35 minutes, cool 5 minutes, and invert to serve.

FLOURLESS CHOCOLATE CAKE

Servings: 8 | Prep: 15m | Cooks: 30m | Total: 1h55m | Additional: 1h10m

NUTRITION FACTS

Calories: 285 | Carbohydrates: 29.9g | Fat: 18.6g | Protein: 4.5g | Cholesterol: 100mg

INGREDIENTS

- 4 (1 ounce) squares semisweet chocolate, chopped
- 1/2 cup cocoa powder
- 1/2 cup butter
- 3 eggs, beaten
- 3/4 cup white sugar

- 1 teaspoon vanilla extract

DIRECTIONS

1. Preheat oven to 300 degrees F (150 degrees C). Grease an 8 inch round cake pan, and dust with cocoa powder.
2. In the top of a double boiler over lightly simmering water, melt chocolate and butter. Remove from heat, and stir in sugar, cocoa powder, eggs, and vanilla. Pour into prepared pan.
3. Bake in preheated oven for 30 minutes. Let cool in pan for 10 minutes, then turn out onto a wire rack and cool completely. Slices can also be reheated for 20 to 30 seconds in the microwave before serving.

SOPAPILLA CHEESECAKE DESSERT

Servings: 12 | Prep: 15m | Cooks: 45m | Total: 3h | Additional: 2h

NUTRITION FACTS

Calories: 553 | Carbohydrates: 50.1g | Fat: 36.2g | Protein: 7.4g | Cholesterol: 82mg

INGREDIENTS

- 3 (8 ounce) packages cream cheese, softened
- 1/2 cup melted butter
- 1 1/2 cups white sugar
- 1/2 cup white sugar
- 1 1/2 teaspoons vanilla extract
- 1 teaspoon ground cinnamon
- 2 (8 ounce) cans crescent roll dough
- 1/4 cup sliced almonds

DIRECTIONS

1. Preheat an oven to 350 degrees F (175 degrees C).
2. Beat the cream cheese with 1 1/2 cups of sugar, and the vanilla extract in a bowl until smooth. Unroll the cans of crescent roll dough, and use a rolling pin to shape the each piece into 9x13 inch rectangles. Press one piece into the bottom of a 9x13 inch baking dish. Evenly spread the cream cheese mixture into the baking dish, then cover with the remaining piece of crescent dough.
3. Drizzle the melted butter evenly over the top of the cheesecake. Stir the remaining 1/2 cup of sugar together with the cinnamon in a small bowl, and sprinkle over the cheesecake along with the almonds.
4. Bake in the preheated oven until the crescent dough has puffed and turned golden brown, about 45 minutes. Cool completely in the pan before cutting into 12 squares.

BUTTERMILK POUND CAKE

Servings: 12 | Prep: 15m | Cooks: 1h30m | Total: 1h45m

NUTRITION FACTS

Calories: 489 | Carbohydrates: 75.1g | Fat: 18.3g | Protein: 7.2g | Cholesterol: 134mg

INGREDIENTS

- 3 cups all-purpose flour
- 6 eggs
- 1/4 teaspoon baking soda
- 1 teaspoon lemon extract
- 1/2 teaspoon salt
- 1 teaspoon vanilla extract
- 1 cup butter
- 1 cup buttermilk
- 3 cups white sugar

DIRECTIONS

1. Preheat oven to 325 degrees F (165 degrees C). Grease one 9 or 10 inch tube pan. Mix together the flour, baking soda, and salt. Set aside.
2. In a large bowl, beat butter with sugar. Mix in the eggs, one at time, beating well after each addition. Stir in the lemon and the vanilla extracts. Gently mix in flour mixture alternately with the buttermilk. Pour batter into the prepared pan.
3. Bake in preheated oven for 90 minutes. Do not open oven door until after one hour. When cake begins to pull away from the side of the pan it is done. Let cool in pan for 10 minutes, then turn out onto a wire rack and cool completely.

MANDARIN ORANGE CAKE

Servings: 18 | Prep: 30m | Cooks: 1h | Total: 2h | Additional: 30m

NUTRITION FACTS

Calories: 337 | Carbohydrates: 38.1g | Fat: 19.9g | Protein: 3g | Cholesterol: 42mg

INGREDIENTS

- 1 (18.25 ounce) package yellow cake mix
- 1 (8 ounce) container frozen whipped topping, thawed
- 4 eggs
- 1 (20 ounce) can crushed pineapple with juice
- 1 cup vegetable oil

- 1 (3.5 ounce) package instant vanilla pudding mix
- 1 (11 ounce) can mandarin orange segments

DIRECTIONS

1. Preheat oven to 350 degrees F (175 degrees C). Grease and flour a 9x13 inch pan.
2. In a large bowl, combine cake mix, eggs, oil and mandarin oranges with juice. Beat until smooth. Pour batter into prepared pan.
3. Bake in the preheated oven for 35 to 40 minutes, or until a toothpick inserted into the center of the cake comes out clean. Allow to cool.
4. To make the topping: In a large bowl, beat together whipped topping, pineapple with juice and dry pudding mix until blended. Spread on cake.

DARK CHOCOLATE CAKE

Servings: 12 | Prep: 20m | Cooks: 35m | Total: 55m

NUTRITION FACTS

Calories: 320 | Carbohydrates: 53.2g | Fat: 11.3g | Protein: 4.9g | Cholesterol: 33mg

INGREDIENTS

- 2 cups all-purpose flour
- 2 eggs
- 2 cups white sugar
- 1 cup cold brewed coffee
- 3/4 cup unsweetened cocoa
- 1 cup milk
- 2 teaspoons baking soda
- 1/2 cup vegetable oil
- 1 teaspoon baking powder
- 2 teaspoons vinegar
- 1/2 teaspoon salt

DIRECTIONS

1. Preheat oven to 350 degrees F (175 degrees C). Grease and flour a 9x13-inch pan.
2. In a large bowl, combine the flour, sugar, cocoa, baking soda, baking powder and salt. Make a well in the center and pour in the eggs, coffee, milk, oil and vinegar. Mix until smooth; the batter will be thin. Pour the batter into the prepared pan.
3. Bake in the preheated oven for 35 to 40 minutes, or until a toothpick inserted into the center of the cake comes out clean. Allow to cool.

BLUEBERRY COFFEE CAKE

Servings: 12 | Prep: 20m | Cooks: 1h | Total: 1h20m

NUTRITION FACTS

Calories: 401 | Carbohydrates: 61.1g | Fat: 16.3g | Protein: 4g | Cholesterol: 57mg

INGREDIENTS

- 1 cup packed brown sugar
- 1/2 cup butter
- 2/3 cup all-purpose flour
- 1 cup white sugar
- 1 teaspoon ground cinnamon
- 1 egg
- 1/2 cup butter
- 1 teaspoon vanilla extract
- 2 cups all-purpose flour
- 1/2 cup milk
- 2 teaspoons baking powder
- 1 cup fresh blueberries
- 1/2 teaspoon salt
- 1/4 cup confectioners' sugar for dusting

DIRECTIONS

1. Heat oven to 350 degrees F (175 degrees C). Coat a Bundt pan well with cooking spray.
2. Make the streusel topping: Mix 1 brown cup sugar, 2/3 cup flour, and cinnamon in a medium bowl. Cut in 1/2 cup butter or margarine; topping mixture will be crumbly. Set aside.
3. For the cake: Beat 1/2 cup butter or margarine in large bowl until creamy; add 1 cup white sugar, and beat until fluffy. Beat in egg and vanilla. Whisk together 2 cups flour, baking powder, and salt; add alternately with the milk to the creamed mixture, beating well after each addition.
4. Spread half the batter in the prepared pan. Cover with berries, and add remaining batter by tablespoons. Cover with streusel topping.
5. Bake at 350 degrees F (175 degrees C) for 55 to 60 minutes, until deep golden brown. Remove pan to wire rack to cool. Invert onto a plate after cake has cooled, and dust with confectioners' sugar.

CARROT PINEAPPLE CAKE

Servings: 24 | Prep: 30m | Cooks: 45m | Total: 1h15m

NUTRITION FACTS

Calories: 329 | Carbohydrates: 37.6g | Fat: 19.1g | Protein: 3.6g | Cholesterol: 39mg

INGREDIENTS

- 2 cups all-purpose flour
- 1 teaspoon vanilla extract
- 2 teaspoons baking soda
- 2 cups shredded carrots
- 1 teaspoon baking powder
- 1 cup flaked coconut
- 1 teaspoon salt
- 1 cup chopped walnuts
- 2 teaspoons ground cinnamon
- 1 (8 ounce) can crushed pineapple, drained
- 1 3/4 cups white sugar
- 1 (8 ounce) package cream cheese
- 1 cup vegetable oil
- 1/4 cup butter, softened
- 3 eggs
- 2 cups confectioners' sugar

DIRECTIONS

1. Preheat oven to 350 degrees F (175 degrees C). Grease and flour a 9x13 inch pan.
2. Mix flour, baking soda, baking powder, salt and cinnamon. Make a well in the center and add sugar, oil, eggs and vanilla. Mix with wooden spoon until smooth. Stir in carrots, coconut, walnuts and pineapple.
3. Pour into 9x13 inch pan. Bake at 350 degrees for about 45 minutes. Don't panic, the center will sink a little. Allow to cool.
4. To make the frosting: Cream the butter and cream cheese until smooth. Add the confectioners sugar and beat until creamy.

PINEAPPLE UPSIDE-DOWN CAKE

Servings: 12 | Prep: 10m | Cooks: 40m | Total: 1h10m | Additional: 20m

NUTRITION FACTS

Calories: 322 | Carbohydrates: 57.7g | Fat: 9.8g | Protein: 2.2g | Cholesterol: 11mg

INGREDIENTS

- 1 (10 ounce) jar maraschino cherries, drained
- 1 (8 ounce) can sliced pineapple, drained with juice reserved
- 1/4 cup butter
- 1 (8 ounce) can crushed pineapple, drained with juice reserved

- 1/2 cup packed brown sugar
- 1 (18.25 ounce) package yellow cake mix
- 1/2 cup flaked coconut

DIRECTIONS

1. Preheat oven to 350 degrees F (175 degrees C). Coat the bottoms and sides of each 9 inch round cake pan with 2 tablespoons of melted butter. Sprinkle the bottom of each pan with 1/4 cup of brown sugar.
2. In one of the pans, sprinkle coconut over the brown sugar. Lay pineapple rings in a single layer on top of coconut. Place a cherry in the center of each ring. In the other pan, spread the drained crushed pineapple.
3. Mix the cake as directed on package, but substitute reserved pineapple juice in place of water. Divide batter between the 2 pans. Remember which pan has the pineapple rings in it.
4. Bake for 40 to 50 minutes in the preheated oven, or until a toothpick inserted into cake comes out clean. Cool in pans for 20 minutes.
5. While the bottoms of the cake pans are still warm to the touch, invert the layer with the crushed pineapple out onto a serving dish, then gently invert the layer with the pineapple rings on top of it for a dazzling two layer pineapple upside down cake.

IRISH CREAM CHOCOLATE CHEESECAKE

Servings: 12 | Prep: 20m | Cooks: 1h20m | Total: 3h20m | Additional: 7h40m

NUTRITION FACTS

Calories: 457 | Carbohydrates: 42.4g | Fat: 29.2g | Protein: 8.1g | Cholesterol: 123mg

INGREDIENTS

- 1 1/2 cups chocolate cookie crumbs
- 1/4 cup unsweetened cocoa powder
- 1/3 cup confectioners' sugar
- 3 tablespoons all-purpose flour
- 1/3 cup unsweetened cocoa powder
- 3 eggs
- 1/4 cup butter
- 1/2 cup sour cream
- 3 (8 ounce) packages cream cheese, softened
- 1/4 cup Irish cream liqueur
- 1 1/4 cups white sugar

DIRECTIONS

1. Preheat oven to 350 degrees F (175 degrees C). In a large bowl, mix together the cookie crumbs, confectioners' sugar and 1/3 cup cocoa. Add melted butter and stir until well mixed. Pat into the bottom of a 9 inch springform pan. Bake in preheated oven for 10 minutes; set aside. Increase oven temperature to 450 degrees F (230 degrees C).
2. In a large bowl, combine cream cheese, white sugar, 1/4 cup cocoa and flour. Beat at medium speed until well blended and smooth. Add eggs one at a time, mixing well after each addition. Blend in the sour cream and Irish cream liqueur; mixing on low speed. Pour filling over baked crust.
3. Bake at 450 degrees F (230 degrees C) for 10 minutes. Reduce oven temperature to 250 degrees F (120 degrees C), and continue baking for 60 minutes.
4. With a knife, loosen cake from rim of pan. Let cool, then remove the rim of pan. Chill before serving. If your cake cracks, a helpful tip is to dampen a spatula and smooth the top, then sprinkle with some chocolate wafer crumbs.

CINNAMON SWIRL BUNDT COFFEE CAKE

Servings: 12 | Prep: 30m | Cooks: 50m | Total: 1h20m

NUTRITION FACTS

Calories: 403 | Carbohydrates: 51.2g | Fat: 20.2g | Protein: 5.8g | Cholesterol: 85mg

INGREDIENTS

- 3/4 cup butter, room temperature
- 1 teaspoon baking soda
- 1 1/2 cups white sugar
- 1 teaspoon baking powder
- 3 eggs
- 1/2 cup chopped walnuts
- 1 teaspoon vanilla extract
- 1 tablespoon ground cinnamon
- 1 cup sour cream
- 1/4 cup white sugar
- 2 1/2 cups all-purpose flour

DIRECTIONS

1. Preheat oven to 400 degrees F (205 degrees C). Grease a 10-inch bundt pan.
2. Beat butter and sugar with an electric mixer in a large bowl until light and fluffy. The mixture should be noticeably lighter in color. Add eggs one at a time, allowing each egg to blend into the butter mixture before adding the next. Mix in vanilla.
3. Combine flour, baking soda, and baking powder. Pour flour mixture into batter alternately with the sour cream, mixing until just incorporated. Fold in walnuts, mixing just enough to evenly combine. Pour half the batter into the prepared pan.

4. Mix the remaining 1/4 cup of white sugar with the cinnamon.
5. Sprinkle cinnamon sugar over the batter in the pan. Drop remaining cake batter in heaping spoonfuls over filling, covering it as best you can.
6. Bake in preheated oven for 8 minutes. Lower heat to 350 degrees F (175 degrees C) and bake for an additional 40 minutes, or until a tester comes out clean.

OMA'S RHUBARB CAKE

Servings: 12 | Prep: 30m | Cooks: 45m | Total: 1h45m

NUTRITION FACTS

Calories: 324 | Carbohydrates: 57.7g | Fat: 9g | Protein: 4.4g | Cholesterol: 50mg

INGREDIENTS

- 1 1/4 cups white sugar
- 3 cups diced rhubarb
- 1 teaspoon baking soda
- 1 cup white sugar
- 1/2 teaspoon salt
- 1/4 cup butter, softened
- 2 cups all-purpose flour
- 1/4 cup all-purpose flour
- 2 eggs, beaten
- ground cinnamon, for dusting
- 1 cup sour cream

DIRECTIONS

1. Preheat the oven to 350 degrees F (175 degrees C). Grease and flour a 9x13 inch baking dish.
2. In a large bowl, stir together 1 1/4 cups sugar, baking soda, salt and 2 cups flour. Stir in the eggs and sour cream until smooth, then fold in the rhubarb. Pour into the prepared dish and spread evenly. In a smaller bowl, stir together the remaining 1 cup sugar and butter until smooth. Stir in 1/4 cup flour until the mixture is crumbly. Sprinkle the mixture on top of the cake then dust lightly with cinnamon.
3. Bake in the preheated oven until a toothpick inserted in the center comes out clean, about 45 minutes.

GA PEACH POUND CAKE

Servings: 16 | Prep: 20m | Cooks: 1h10m | Total: 1h30m

NUTRITION FACTS

Calories: 307 | Carbohydrates: 44.1g | Fat: 13g | Protein: 4.1g | Cholesterol: 77mg

INGREDIENTS

- 1 cup butter or margarine, softened
- 3 cups all-purpose flour
- 2 cups white sugar
- 1 teaspoon baking powder
- 4 eggs
- 1/2 teaspoon salt
- 1 teaspoon vanilla extract
- 2 cups fresh peaches, pitted and chopped

DIRECTIONS

1. Preheat oven to 325 degrees F (165 degrees C). Butter a 10 inch tube pan and coat with white sugar.
2. In a large bowl, cream together the butter and sugar until light and fluffy. Add the eggs one at a time, beating well with each addition, then stir in the vanilla. Reserve 1/4 cup of flour for later, and sift together the remaining flour, baking powder and salt. Gradually stir into the creamed mixture. Use the reserved flour to coat the chopped peaches, then fold the floured peaches into the batter. Spread evenly into the prepared pan.
3. Bake for 60 to 70 minutes in the preheated oven, or until a toothpick inserted into the cake comes out clean. Allow cake to cool in the pan for 10 minutes, before inverting onto a wire rack to cool completely.

GRANDMOTHER'S POUND CAKE

Servings: 30 | Prep: 30m | Cooks: 1h10m | Total: 1h40m

NUTRITION FACTS

Calories: 264 | Carbohydrates: 33.1g | Fat: 13.5g | Protein: 3.3g | Cholesterol: 70mg

INGREDIENTS

- 2 cups butter
- 4 cups all-purpose flour
- 3 cups white sugar
- 2/3 cup milk
- 6 eggs

DIRECTIONS

1. Preheat oven to 350 degrees F (175 degrees C). Grease 3 - 8x4 inch loaf pans, then line with parchment paper.

2. In a large bowl, cream together the butter and sugar until light and fluffy. Beat in the eggs one at a time. Beat in the flour alternately with the milk, mixing just until incorporated.
3. Pour batter evenly into prepared loaf pans. Bake in the preheated oven for 70 minutes, or until a toothpick inserted into the center of the cakes comes out clean. After removing them from the oven, immediately loosen cake edges with a knife. Allow to cool in pans for 10 minutes, then remove from the pans. Strip off the parchment paper and cool completely on wire racks.

MINI CHEESECAKES

Servings: 6 | Prep: 20m | Cooks: 25m | Total: 1h15m | Additional: 30m

NUTRITION FACTS

Calories: 219 | Carbohydrates: 15.2g | Fat: 16.1g | Protein: 4.2g | Cholesterol: 72mg

INGREDIENTS

- 1/3 cup graham cracker crumbs
- 1 1/2 teaspoons lemon juice
- 1 tablespoon white sugar
- 1/2 teaspoon grated lemon zest
- 1 tablespoon margarine, melte
- 1/4 teaspoon vanilla extract
- 1 (8 ounce) package cream cheese, softened
- 1 egg
- 1/4 cup white sugar

DIRECTIONS

1. Preheat oven to 325 degrees F (165 degrees C). Grease a 6-cup muffin pan.
2. In a medium bowl, mix together the graham cracker crumbs, sugar, and margarine with a fork until combined. Measure a rounded tablespoon of the mixture into the bottom of each muffin cup, pressing firmly. Bake in the pre-heated oven for 5 minutes, then remove to cool. Keep the oven on.
3. Beat together the cream cheese, sugar, lemon juice, lemon zest and vanilla until fluffy. Mix in the egg.
4. Pour the cream cheese mixture into the muffin cups, filling each until 3/4 full. Bake at 325 degrees F (165 degrees C) for 25 minutes. Cool completely in pan before removing. Refrigerate until ready to serve.

RED VELVET CAKE

Servings: 12 | Prep: 25m | Cooks: 30m | Total: 2h25m | Additional: 1h30m

NUTRITION FACTS

Calories: 513 | Carbohydrates: 66.6g | Fat: 25.7g | Protein: 5.8g | Cholesterol: 74mg

INGREDIENTS

- 1/2 cup shortening
- 2 1/2 cups sifted all-purpose flour
- 1 1/2 cups white sugar
- 1 1/2 teaspoons baking soda
- 2 eggs
- 1 tablespoon distilled white vinegar
- 2 tablespoons cocoa
- 5 tablespoons all-purpose flour
- 4 tablespoons red food coloring
- 1 cup milk
- 1 teaspoon salt
- 1 cup white sugar
- 1 teaspoon vanilla extract
- 1 cup butter, room temperature
- 1 cup buttermilk
- 1 teaspoon vanilla extract

DIRECTIONS

1. Preheat oven to 350 degrees F (175 degrees C). Grease two 9-inch round pans.
2. Beat shortening and 1 1/2 cups sugar until very light and fluffy. Add eggs and beat well.
3. Make a paste of cocoa and red food coloring; add to creamed mixture. Mix salt, 1 teaspoon vanilla, and buttermilk together. Add the flour to the batter, alternating with the buttermilk mixture, mixing just until incorporated. Mix soda and vinegar and gently fold into cake batter. Don't beat or stir the batter after this point.
4. Pour batter into prepared pans. Bake in preheated oven until a tester inserted into the cake comes out clean, about 30 minutes. Cool cakes completely on wire rack.
5. To Make Icing: Cook 5 tablespoons flour and milk over low heat till thick, stirring constantly. Let cool completely! While mixture is cooling, beat 1 cup sugar, butter, and 1 teaspoon vanilla until light and fluffy. Add cooled flour mixture and beat until frosting is a good spreading consistency. Frost cake layers when completely cool.

PINEAPPLE UPSIDE-DOWN CAKE

Servings: 12 | Prep: 10m | Cooks: 40m | Total: 1h10m | Additional: 20m

NUTRITION FACTS

Calories: 322 | Carbohydrates: 57.7g | Fat:9.8g | Protein: 2.2g | Cholesterol: 11mg

INGREDIENTS

- 1 (10 ounce) jar maraschino cherries, drained
- 1 (8 ounce) can sliced pineapple, drained with juice reserved
- 1/4 cup butter
- 1 (8 ounce) can crushed pineapple, drained with juice reserved
- 1/2 cup packed brown sugar
- 1 (18.25 ounce) package yellow cake mix
- 1/2 cup flaked coconut

DIRECTIONS

1. Preheat oven to 350 degrees F (175 degrees C). Coat the bottoms and sides of each 9 inch round cake pan with 2 tablespoons of melted butter. Sprinkle the bottom of each pan with 1/4 cup of brown sugar.
2. In one of the pans, sprinkle coconut over the brown sugar. Lay pineapple rings in a single layer on top of coconut. Place a cherry in the center of each ring. In the other pan, spread the drained crushed pineapple.
3. Mix the cake as directed on package, but substitute reserved pineapple juice in place of water. Divide batter between the 2 pans. Remember which pan has the pineapple rings in it.
4. Bake for 40 to 50 minutes in the preheated oven, or until a toothpick inserted into cake comes out clean. Cool in pans for 20 minutes.
5. While the bottoms of the cake pans are still warm to the touch, invert the layer with the crushed pineapple out onto a serving dish, then gently invert the layer with the pineapple rings on top of it for a dazzling two layer pineapple upside down cake.

IRISH CREAM CHOCOLATE CHEESECAKE

Servings: 12 | Prep: 20m | Cooks: 1h20m | Total: 9h20m | Additional: 7h40m

NUTRITION FACTS

Calories: 457 | Carbohydrates: 42.4g | Fat: 29.2g | Protein: 8.1g | Cholesterol: 123mg

INGREDIENTS

- 1 1/2 cups chocolate cookie crumbs
- 1/4 cup unsweetened cocoa powder
- 1/3 cup confectioners' sugar
- 3 tablespoons all-purpose flour
- 1/3 cup unsweetened cocoa powder
- 3 eggs
- 1/4 cup butter
- 1/2 cup sour cream

- 3 (8 ounce) packages cream cheese, softened
- 1/4 cup Irish cream liqueur
- 1 1/4 cups white sugar

DIRECTIONS

1. Preheat oven to 350 degrees F (175 degrees C). In a large bowl, mix together the cookie crumbs, confectioners' sugar and 1/3 cup cocoa. Add melted butter and stir until well mixed. Pat into the bottom of a 9 inch springform pan. Bake in preheated oven for 10 minutes; set aside. Increase oven temperature to 450 degrees F (230 degrees C).
2. In a large bowl, combine cream cheese, white sugar, 1/4 cup cocoa and flour. Beat at medium speed until well blended and smooth. Add eggs one at a time, mixing well after each addition. Blend in the sour cream and Irish cream liqueur; mixing on low speed. Pour filling over baked crust.
3. Bake at 450 degrees F (230 degrees C) for 10 minutes. Reduce oven temperature to 250 degrees F (120 degrees C), and continue baking for 60 minutes.
4. With a knife, loosen cake from rim of pan. Let cool, then remove the rim of pan. Chill before serving. If your cake cracks, a helpful tip is to dampen a spatula and smooth the top, then sprinkle with some chocolate wafer crumbs.

CINNAMON SWIRL BUNDT COFFEE CAKE

Servings: 12 | Prep: 30m | Cooks: 50m | Total: 1h20m

NUTRITION FACTS

Calories: 403 | Carbohydrates: 51.2g | Fat: 20.2g | Protein: 5.8g | Cholesterol: 85mg

INGREDIENTS

- 3/4 cup butter, room temperature
- 1 teaspoon baking soda
- 1 1/2 cups white sugar
- 1 teaspoon baking powder
- 3 eggs
- 1/2 cup chopped walnuts
- 1 teaspoon vanilla extract
- 1 tablespoon ground cinnamon
- 1 cup sour cream
- 1/4 cup white sugar
- 2 1/2 cups all-purpose flour

DIRECTIONS

1. Preheat oven to 400 degrees F (205 degrees C). Grease a 10-inch bundt pan.

2. Beat butter and sugar with an electric mixer in a large bowl until light and fluffy. The mixture should be noticeably lighter in color. Add eggs one at a time, allowing each egg to blend into the butter mixture before adding the next. Mix in vanilla.
3. Combine flour, baking soda, and baking powder. Pour flour mixture into batter alternately with the sour cream, mixing until just incorporated. Fold in walnuts, mixing just enough to evenly combine. Pour half the batter into the prepared pan.
4. Mix the remaining 1/4 cup of white sugar with the cinnamon.
5. Sprinkle cinnamon sugar over the batter in the pan. Drop remaining cake batter in heaping spoonfuls over filling, covering it as best you can.
6. Bake in preheated oven for 8 minutes. Lower heat to 350 degrees F (175 degrees C) and bake for an additional 40 minutes, or until a tester comes out clean.

OMA'S RHUBARB CAKE

Servings: 12 | Prep: 30m | Cooks: 45m | Total: 1h15m

NUTRITION FACTS

Calories: 324 | Carbohydrates: 57.7g | Fat: 9g | Protein: 4.4g | Cholesterol: 50mg

INGREDIENTS

- 1 1/4 cups white sugar
- 3 cups diced rhubarb
- 1 teaspoon baking soda
- 1 cup white sugar
- 1/2 teaspoon salt
- 1/4 cup butter, softened
- 2 cups all-purpose flour
- 1/4 cup all-purpose flour
- 2 eggs, beaten
- ground cinnamon, for dusting
- 1 cup sour cream

DIRECTIONS

1. Preheat the oven to 350 degrees F (175 degrees C). Grease and flour a 9x13 inch baking dish.
2. In a large bowl, stir together 1 1/4 cups sugar, baking soda, salt and 2 cups flour. Stir in the eggs and sour cream until smooth, then fold in the rhubarb. Pour into the prepared dish and spread evenly. In a smaller bowl, stir together the remaining 1 cup sugar and butter until smooth. Stir in 1/4 cup flour until the mixture is crumbly. Sprinkle the mixture on top of the cake then dust lightly with cinnamon.
3. Bake in the preheated oven until a toothpick inserted in the center comes out clean, about 45 minutes.

GA PEACH POUND CAKE

Servings: 16 | Prep: 20m | Cooks: 1h10m | Total: 1h30m

NUTRITION FACTS

Calories: 307 | Carbohydrates: 44.1g | Fat: 13g | Protein: 4.1g | Cholesterol: 77mg

INGREDIENTS

- 1 cup butter or margarine, softened
- 3 cups all-purpose flour
- 2 cups white sugar
- 1 teaspoon baking powder
- 4 eggs
- 1/2 teaspoon salt
- 1 teaspoon vanilla extract
- 2 cups fresh peaches, pitted and chopped

DIRECTIONS

1. Preheat oven to 325 degrees F (165 degrees C). Butter a 10 inch tube pan and coat with white sugar.
2. In a large bowl, cream together the butter and sugar until light and fluffy. Add the eggs one at a time, beating well with each addition, then stir in the vanilla. Reserve 1/4 cup of flour for later, and sift together the remaining flour, baking powder and salt. Gradually stir into the creamed mixture. Use the reserved flour to coat the chopped peaches, then fold the floured peaches into the batter. Spread evenly into the prepared pan.
3. Bake for 60 to 70 minutes in the preheated oven, or until a toothpick inserted into the cake comes out clean. Allow cake to cool in the pan for 10 minutes, before inverting onto a wire rack to cool completely.

PUMPKIN SPICE CUPCAKES

Servings: 24 | Prep: 25m | Cooks: 25m | Total: 1h40m | Additional: 50m

NUTRITION FACTS

Calories: 244 | Carbohydrates: 37.2g | Fat: 9.8g | Protein: 2.9g | Cholesterol: 42mg

INGREDIENTS

- 21/4 cups all-purpose flour
- 1 cup white sugar
- 1 teaspoon ground cinnamon
- 1/3 cup brown sugar
- 1/2 teaspoon ground nutmeg

- 2 eggs, room temperature
- 1/2 teaspoon ground ginger
- 3/4 cup milk
- 1/2 teaspoon ground cloves
- 1 cup pumpkin puree
- 1/2 teaspoon ground allspice
- 1 (8 ounce) package cream cheese, softened
- 1/2 teaspoon salt
- 1/4 cup butter, softened
- 1 tablespoon baking powder
- 3 cups confectioners' sugar
- 1/2 teaspoon baking soda
- 1 teaspoon vanilla extract
- 1/2 cup butter, softened
- 1 teaspoon ground cinnamon

DIRECTIONS

1. Preheat an oven to 375 degrees F (190 degrees C). Grease 24 muffin cups, or line with paper muffin liners. Sift together the flour, 1 teaspoon cinnamon, nutmeg, ginger, clove, allspice, salt, baking powder, and baking soda; set aside.
2. Beat 1/2 cup of butter, the white sugar, and brown sugar with an electric mixer in a large bowl until light and fluffy. The mixture should be noticeably lighter in color. Add the room-temperature eggs one at a time, allowing each egg to blend into the butter mixture before adding the next. Stir in the milk and pumpkin puree after the last egg. Stir in the flour mixture, mixing until just incorporated. Pour the batter into the prepared muffin cups.
3. Bake in the preheated oven until golden and the tops spring back when lightly pressed, about 25 minutes. Cool in the pans for 5 minutes before removing to cool completely on a wire rack.
4. While the cupcakes are cooling, make the frosting by beating the cream cheese and 1/4 butter with an electric mixer in a bowl until smooth. Beat in the confectioners' sugar a little at a time until incorporated. Add the vanilla extract and 1 teaspoon ground cinnamon; beat until fluffy. Once the cupcakes are cool, frost with the cream cheese icing.

CARROT CUPCAKES WITH WHITE CHOCOLATE CREAM CHEESE ICING

Servings: 12 | Prep: 30m | Cooks: 25m | Total: 1h55m | Additional: 1h

NUTRITION FACTS

Calories: 639 | Carbohydrates: 84.7g | Fat: 32.2g | Protein: 6g | Cholesterol: 76mg

INGREDIENTS

- 2 ounces white chocolate
- 1/2 cup vegetable oil
- 1 (8 ounce) package cream cheese, softened
- 1 teaspoon vanilla extract
- 1/2 cup unsalted butter, softened
- 2 cups shredded carrots
- 1 teaspoon vanilla extract
- 1/2 cup crushed pineapple
- 1/2 teaspoon orange extract
- 1 1/2 cups all-purpose flour
- 4 cups confectioners' sugar
- 1 1/4 teaspoons baking soda
- 2 tablespoons heavy cream
- 1/2 teaspoon salt
- 2 eggs, lightly beaten
- 1 1/2 teaspoons ground cinnamon
- 1 1/8 cups white sugar
- 1/2 teaspoon ground nutmeg
- 1/3 cup brown sugar
- 1/4 teaspoon ground ginger
- 1 cup chopped walnuts

DIRECTIONS

1. Preheat oven to 350 degrees F (175 degrees C). Lightly grease 12 muffin cups.
2. In small saucepan, melt white chocolate over low heat. Stir until smooth, and allow to cool to room temperature.
3. In a bowl, beat together the cream cheese and butter until smooth. Mix in white chocolate, 1 teaspoon vanilla, and orange extract. Gradually beat in the confectioners' sugar until the mixture is fluffy. Mix in heavy cream.
4. Beat together the eggs, white sugar, and brown sugar in a bowl, and mix in the oil and vanilla. Fold in carrots and pineapple. In a separate bowl, mix the flour, baking soda, salt, cinnamon, nutmeg, and ginger. Mix flour mixture into the carrot mixture until evenly moist. Fold in 1/2 cup walnuts. Transfer to the prepared muffin cups.
5. Bake 25 minutes in the preheated oven, or until a toothpick inserted in the center of a muffin comes out clean. Cool completely on wire racks before topping with the icing and sprinkling with remaining walnuts.

PUMPKIN CRUMB CAKE

Servings: 18 | Prep: 15m | Cooks: 45m | Total: 1h

NUTRITION FACTS

Calories: 287 | Carbohydrates: 39.2g | Fat: 13.7g | Protein: 3.5g | Cholesterol: 61mg

INGREDIENTS

- 1 (18.25 ounce) package yellow cake mix
- 1/4 cup packed brown sugar
- 1 egg, beaten
- 1 1/2 teaspoons ground cinnamon
- 1/2 cup butter, melted
- 1/2 cup white sugar
- 1 (15 ounce) can pumpkin puree
- 3 tablespoons butter, softened
- 3 eggs, beaten
- 1/2 cup chopped nuts (optional)
- 1/2 cup white sugar

DIRECTIONS

1. Preheat oven to 350 degrees F (175 degrees C). Spray or grease one 9x13 inch pan.
2. Reserve 1 cup cake mix. In a large bowl, combine the remaining dry cake mix with 1 egg and 1/2 cup melted butter. Mix well, and then pat into prepared pan.
3. In a large bowl, mix together the pumpkin, 3 eggs, 1/2 cup white sugar, brown sugar, and cinnamon. Pour over crust.
4. In a small bowl, combine reserved 1 cup cake mix, 1/2 cup sugar, and 3 tablespoons softened butter. Crumble over pumpkin filling. Sprinkle nuts evenly over the top, if desired.
5. Bake in preheated oven for 40 to 45 minutes.

COCONUT CREAM CAKE

Servings: 24 | Prep: 15m | Cooks: 35m | Total: 8h50m | Additional: 8h

NUTRITION FACTS

Calories: 288 | Carbohydrates: 36.6g | Fat: 14.6g | Protein: 3.5g | Cholesterol: 42mg

INGREDIENTS

- 1 (18.25 ounce) package white cake mix
- 1 (14 ounce) can sweetened cream of coconut
- 3 eggs
- 1 (14 ounce) can sweetened condensed milk
- 1/3 cup vegetable oil
- 1 cup heavy whipping cream
- 1 cup water
- 1 tablespoon white sugar

- 1/2 teaspoon coconut extract
- 1 cup flaked coconut

DIRECTIONS

1. Preheat oven to 350 degrees F (175 degrees C). Grease and flour a 9x13 inch pan.
2. In a large bowl, mix together cake mix, eggs, oil, water and coconut flavoring. Beat for 2 minutes and pour into 9x13 inch pan. Bake for 30 minutes, or until a toothpick inserted into the cake comes out clean.
3. In a medium bowl, combine coconut cream with sweetened condensed milk and stir until smooth. When cake comes out of the oven, poke holes into it in even rows using a large fork or chopsticks. Pour milk mixture over, allowing it to soak into the cake. Refrigerate for several hours or overnight.
4. In a large bowl, whisk cream until soft peaks form. Add sugar and continue whipping until stiff. Spread over cooled cake. Sprinkle top with flaked coconut.

LEMON CUPCAKES

Servings: 30 | Prep: 48m | Cooks: 17m | Total: 1h25m | Additional: 20m

NUTRITION FACTS

Calories: 232 | Carbohydrates: 26.7g | Fat: 13.1g | Protein: 2.7g | Cholesterol: 64mg

INGREDIENTS

- 3 cups self-rising flour
- 2 tablespoons lemon zest
- 1/2 teaspoon salt
- 1 cup whole milk, divided
- 1 cup unsalted butter, at room temperature
- 2 1/2 tablespoons fresh lemon juice, divided
- 2 cups white sugar
- 2 cups chilled heavy cream
- 4 eggs, at room temperature
- 3/4 cup confectioners' sugar
- 1 teaspoon vanilla extract
- 1 1/2 tablespoons fresh lemon juice

DIRECTIONS

1. Preheat oven to 375 degrees F (190 degrees C). Line 30 cupcake pan cups with paper liners.
2. Sift the self-rising flour and salt together in a bowl. In another bowl, beat the unsalted butter and sugar with an electric mixer until light and fluffy. Beat in the eggs one at a time, beating each egg until incorporated before adding the next. Mix in the vanilla extract and lemon zest.

3. Gently beat the flour mixture into the butter mixture, one third at a time, alternating with half the milk and half the lemon juice after each of the first 2 additions of flour. Beat until just combined; do not over mix.
4. Fill the prepared cupcake liners with batter 3/4 full, and bake in the preheated oven until a toothpick inserted in the center comes out clean, about 17 minutes. Let the cupcakes cool in the pans for about 10 minutes before removing them to finish cooling on a rack.
5. To make the icing, beat the cream in a chilled bowl with an electric mixer set on Low until the cream begins to thicken. Add the confectioners' sugar and lemon juice, a little at a time, beating after each addition, until fully incorporated. Increase the mixer speed to High, and beat until the icing forms soft peaks, about 5 minutes. Spread on the cooled cupcakes. Refrigerate leftovers.

NO-BAKE CHOCOLATE ECLAIR CAKE

Servings: 12 | Prep: 20m | Cooks: 3m | Total: 2h25m | Additional: 2h2m

NUTRITION FACTS

Calories: 414 | Carbohydrates: 65.2g | Fat: 15.4g | Protein: 4.8g | Cholesterol: 10mg

INGREDIENTS

- 2 (3 ounce) packages instant vanilla pudding mix
- 1/3 cup unsweetened cocoa powder
- 3 cups milk
- 1 cup white sugar
- 1 (8 ounce) container frozen whipped topping, thawed
- 2 tablespoons butter
- 1 (16 ounce) package chocolate graham crackers
- 1 teaspoon vanilla extract
- 1/4 cup milk

DIRECTIONS

1. In a large bowl, combine pudding mix and 3 cups milk; mix well. Fold in whipped topping and beat with mixer for 2 minutes.
2. In a buttered 9x13 inch baking dish, spread a layer of graham crackers on the bottom of the dish.
3. Spread 1/2 of the pudding mixture over crackers, then top with graham crackers. Spread remaining pudding over crackers; top second pudding layer with another layer of crackers.
4. To make topping: In a medium saucepan over medium-high heat, combine 1/4 cup milk, cocoa and sugar and allow to boil for 1 minute; remove from heat and add butter and vanilla. Mix well and cool.
5. Pour sauce over graham cracker layer and refrigerate until set; serve.

BROWNIE CARAMEL CHEESECAKE

Servings: 12 | Prep: 30m | Cooks: 1hm | Total: 4h30m | Additional: 3h

NUTRITION FACTS

Calories: 512 | Carbohydrates: 68.9g | Fat: 24.1g | Protein: 8.2g | Cholesterol: 93mg

INGREDIENTS

- 1 (9 ounce) package brownie mix
- 2 (8 ounce) packages cream cheese, softened
- 1 egg
- 1/2 cup white sugar
- 1 tablespoon cold water
- 1 teaspoon vanilla extract
- 1 (14 ounce) package individually wrapped caramels, unwrapped
- 2 eggs
- 1 (5 ounce) can evaporated milk
- 1 cup chocolate fudge topping

DIRECTIONS

1. Preheat oven to 350 degrees F (175 degrees C). Grease the bottom of a 9 inch springform pan.
2. In a small bowl, mix together brownie mix, 1 egg and water. Spread into the greased pan. Bake for 25 minutes.
3. Melt the caramels with the evaporated milk over low heat in a heavy saucepan. Stir often, and heat until mixture has a smooth consistency. Reserve 1/3 cup of this caramel mixture, and pour the remainder over the warm, baked brownie crust.
4. In a large bowl, beat the cream cheese, sugar and vanilla with an electric mixer until smooth. Add eggs one at a time, beating well after each addition. Pour cream cheese mixture over caramel mixture.
5. Bake cheesecake for 40 minutes. Chill in pan. When cake is thoroughly chilled, loosen by running a knife around the edge, and then remove the rim of the pan. Heat reserved caramel mixture, and spoon over cheesecake. Drizzle with the chocolate topping.

STRAWBERRY SHORTCAKE

Servings: 8 | Prep: 30m | Cooks: 20m | Total: 50m

NUTRITION FACTS

Calories: 430 | Carbohydrates: 55.2g | Fat: 21.4g | Protein: 6.6g | Cholesterol: 66mg

INGREDIENTS

- 3 pints fresh strawberries
- 1/4 teaspoon salt
- 1/2 cup white sugar
- 1/3 cup shortening
- 2 1/4 cups all-purpose flour
- 1 egg
- 4 teaspoons baking powder
- 2/3 cup milk
- 2 tablespoons white sugar
- 2 cups whipped heavy cream

DIRECTIONS

1. Slice the strawberries and toss them with 1/2 cup of white sugar. Set aside.
2. Preheat oven to 425 degrees F (220 degrees C). Grease and flour one 8 inch round cake pan.
3. In a medium bowl combine the flour, baking powder, 2 tablespoons white sugar and the salt. With a pastry blender cut in the shortening until the mixture resembles coarse crumbs. Make a well in the center and add the beaten egg and milk. Stir until just combined.
4. Spread the batter into the prepared pan. Bake at 425 degrees F (220 degrees C) for 15 to 20 minutes or until golden brown. Let cool partially in pan on wire rack.
5. Slice partially cooled cake in half, making two layers. Place half of the strawberries on one layer and top with the other layer. Top with remaining strawberries and cover with the whipped cream.

TWO INGREDIENT PUMPKIN CAKE

Servings: 15 | Prep: 5m | Cooks: 25m | Total: 30m

NUTRITION FACTS

Calories: 157 | Carbohydrates: 27.5g | Fat: 4.3g | Protein: 2.4g | Cholesterol: 0mg

INGREDIENTS

- 1 (18.25 ounce) package spice cake mix
- 1 (15 ounce) can pumpkin

DIRECTIONS

1. Preheat the oven to 350 degrees F (175 degrees C). Generously grease a 9x13 inch baking pan.
2. In a large bowl, mix together the spice cake mix and canned pumpkin until well blended. Spread evenly into the prepared pan.
3. Bake for 25 to 30 minutes in the preheated oven, or until a knife inserted into the center comes out clean. Cool and serve, or store in the refrigerator. This tastes even better the next day.

EGGNOG CHEESECAKE

Servings: 16 | Prep: 30m | Cooks: 55m | Total: 1h25m

NUTRITION FACTS

Calories: 277 | Carbohydrates: 22g | Fat: 18.9g | Protein: 5g | Cholesterol: 82mg

INGREDIENTS

- 1 cup graham cracker crumbs
- 3 tablespoons all-purpose flour
- 2 tablespoons white sugar
- 3/4 cup eggnog
- 3 tablespoons melted butter
- 2 eggs
- 3 (8 ounce) packages cream cheese, softened
- 2 tablespoons rum
- 1 cup white sugar
- 1 pinch ground nutmeg

DIRECTIONS

1. Preheat oven to 325 degrees F (165 degrees C).
2. In a medium bowl combine graham cracker crumbs, 2 tablespoons sugar and butter. Press into the bottom of a 9 inch spring form pan.
3. Bake in preheated oven for 10 minutes. Place on a wire rack to cool.
4. Preheat oven to 425 degrees F (220 degrees C).
5. in a food processor combine cream cheese, 1 cup sugar, flour and eggnog; process until smooth. Blend in eggs, rum and nutmeg. Pour mixture into cooled crust.
6. Bake in preheated oven for 10 minutes.
7. Reduce heat to 250 and bake for 45 minutes, or until center of cake is barely firm to the touch. Remove from the oven and immediately loosen cake from rim. Let cake cool completely before removing the rim.

CARAMEL MACCHIATO CHEESECAKE

Servings: 12 | Prep: 35m | Cooks: 1h28m | Total: 10h3m | Additional: 8h

NUTRITION FACTS

Calories: 486 | Carbohydrates: 37.1g | Fat: 35g | Protein: 7.7g | Cholesterol: 141mg

INGREDIENTS

- 2 cups graham cracker crumbs

- 1 (8 ounce) container sour cream
- 1/2 cup butter, melted
- 1 (8 ounce) container sour cream
- 2 tablespoons white sugar
- 2 teaspoons vanilla extract
- 3 (8 ounce) packages cream cheese, softened
- pressurized whipped cream
- 1 cup white sugar
- caramel ice cream topping
- 3 eggs

DIRECTIONS

1. Preheat oven to 350 degrees F (175 degrees C). Lightly coat a 9-inch springform pan with nonstick cooking spray.
2. Mix together the graham cracker crumbs, melted butter, and 2 tablespoons of sugar until well combined. Press into the bottom of the prepared springform pan, and 1 inch up the sides. Bake in preheated oven for 8 minutes, then remove to cool on a wire rack.
3. Reduce oven temperature to 325 degrees F (165 degrees C).
4. Beat the softened cream cheese in a large bowl with an electric mixer until fluffy. Gradually add 1 cup of sugar, beating until blended. Add eggs one at a time, beating well after each addition. Stir in sour cream, espresso and vanilla. Pour batter into the baked and cooled crust.
5. Bake cheesecake in the preheated oven for 1 hour and 5 minutes; then turn the oven off, partially open the door and allow the cheesecake to rest for 15 minutes more. Remove from the oven, and run a knife around the edges. Cool cheesecake on a wire rack to room temperature, then cover the springform pan with plastic wrap, and chill in the refrigerator for 8 hours.
6. To serve, cut the cheesecake into wedges and garnish each slice with whipped cream and caramel sauce.

LEMON CAKE WITH LEMON FILLING AND LEMON BUTTER FROSTING

Servings: 12 | Prep: 1h | Cooks: 1h | Total: 4h | Additional: 2h

NUTRITION FACTS

Calories: 601 | Carbohydrates: 92.5g | Fat: 24.5g | Protein: 5.6g | Cholesterol: 173mg

INGREDIENTS

- 2 cups all-purpose flour
- 1 tablespoon cornstarch
- 2 teaspoons baking powder
- 6 tablespoons butter

- 1 teaspoon salt
- 3/4 cup white sugar
- 1/2 cup butter
- 4 egg yolks, beaten
- 1 1/4 cups white sugar
- 4 cups confectioners' sugar
- 3 eggs
- 1/2 cup butter, softened
- 1 teaspoon vanilla extract
- 2 tablespoons fresh lemon juice
- 1 cup milk
- 1 teaspoon grated lemon zest
- 1 tablespoon grated lemon zest
- 2 tablespoons milk
- 1/2 cup fresh lemon juice

DIRECTIONS

1. Preheat oven to 350 degrees F (175 degrees C). Grease and flour two 8 inch round pans. Mix together the flour, baking powder and salt. Set aside
2. In a large bowl, cream together the butter and sugar until light and fluffy, about 5 minutes. Beat in the eggs one at a time, then stir in the vanilla. Beat in the flour mixture alternately with the milk, mixing just until incorporated.
3. Pour batter into prepared pans. Bake in the preheated oven for 30 minutes, or until a toothpick inserted into the center of the cake comes out clean. Allow to cool in pans on wire racks for 10 minutes. Then invert onto wire racks to cool completely.
4. To make filling: In medium saucepan, mix together 1 tablespoon lemon zest, 1/2 cup lemon juice and 1 tablespoon cornstarch until smooth. Mix in 6 tablespoons butter and 3/4 cup sugar, and bring mixture to boil over medium heat. Boil for one minute, stirring constantly. In small bowl, with a wire whisk, beat egg yolks until smooth. Whisk in a small amount of the hot lemon mixture. Pour the egg mixture into the sauce pan, beating the hot lemon mixture rapidly. Reduce heat to low; cook, stirring constantly, 5 minutes, or until thick (not to boil).
5. Pour mixture into medium bowl. Press plastic wrap onto surface to keep skin from forming as it cools. Cool to room temperature. Refrigerate 3 hours.
6. To make frosting: In large bowl, beat confectioners' sugar, 1/2 cup butter, 2 tablespoons lemon juice and 1 teaspoon lemon zest until smooth. Beat in milk, and increase speed and continue to beat until light and fluffy.
7. To assemble: With long serrated knife, split each cake layer in half horizontally, making 4 layers. Place 1 layer, cut side up, on a serving plate. Spread with half of the lemon filling. Top with another layer, and spread with 1/2 cup frosting. Add third layer, and spread with remaining half of the lemon filling. Press on final cake layer, and frost top and sides of cake with remaining frosting. Refrigerate cake until serving time.

MINI CHEESECAKES

Servings: 12 | Prep: 25m | Cooks: 15m | Total: 1h40m | Additional: 1h

NUTRITION FACTS

Calories: 271 | Carbohydrates: 30.5g | Fat: 15g | Protein: 4.3g | Cholesterol: 72mg

INGREDIENTS

- 12 vanilla wafers
- 2 tablespoons lemon juice
- 2 (8 ounce) packages cream cheese, softened
- 2/3 cup white sugar
- 2 eggs
- 1 (21 ounce) can cherry pie filling, or flavor of choice

DIRECTIONS

1. Preheat oven to 350 degrees F (175 degrees C).
2. Line muffin tins with 12 paper baking cups. Place a vanilla wafer in each one.
3. In a medium mixing bowl beat cream cheese until fluffy. Add eggs, lemon juice, and sugar. Beat until smooth and thoroughly combined.
4. Fill each baking cup 2/3 full with cream cheese mixture.
5. Bake in preheated oven for 15 to 17 minutes. Cool on a rack. Top with fruit pie filling. Pipe whipped cream or sweetened cream cheese into a rosette on top of each cheesecake just prior to serving, if desired.

APPLE CINNAMON WHITE CAKE

Servings: 12 | Prep: 20m | Cooks: 30m | Total: 50m

NUTRITION FACTS

Calories: 208 | Carbohydrates: 29.5g | Fat: 8.9g | Protein: 3.1g | Cholesterol: 52mg

INGREDIENTS

- 1/3 cup brown sugar
- 1 1/2 teaspoons vanilla extract
- 1 teaspoon ground cinnamon
- 1 1/2 cups all-purpose flour
- 2/3 cup white sugar
- 1 3/4 teaspoons baking powder
- 1/2 cup butter, softened
- 1/2 cup milk

- 2 eggs
- 1 apple, peeled and chopped

DIRECTIONS

1. Preheat oven to 350 degrees F (175 degrees C). Grease and flour a 9x5-inch loaf pan.
2. Mix brown sugar and cinnamon together in a bowl.
3. Beat white sugar and butter together in a bowl using an electric mixer until smooth and creamy. Beat in eggs, 1 at a time, until incorporated; add vanilla extract.
4. Combine flour and baking powder together in a bowl; stir into creamed butter mixture. Mix milk into batter until smooth. Pour half the batter into the prepared loaf pan; add half the apples and half the brown sugar mixture. Lightly pat apple mixture into batter. Pour the remaining batter over apple layer; top with remaining apples and brown sugar mixture. Lightly pat apples into batter; swirl brown sugar mixture through apples using a finger or spoon.
5. Bake in the preheated oven until a toothpick inserted in the center of the loaf comes out clean, 30 to 40 minutes.

ANGEL FOOD CAKE

Servings: 14 | Prep: 30m | Cooks: 45m | Total: 1h15m

NUTRITION FACTS

Calories: 136 | Carbohydrates: 29.9g | Fat: 0.1g | Protein: 4g | Cholesterol: 0mg

INGREDIENTS

- 1 cup cake flour
- 1 1/2 teaspoons vanilla extract
- 1 1/2 cups white sugar
- 1 ½ teaspoons cream of tartar
- 12 egg whites
- 1/2 teaspoon salt

DIRECTIONS

1. Preheat the oven to 375 degrees F (190 degrees C). Be sure that your 10 inch tube pan is clean and dry. Any amount of oil or residue could deflate the egg whites. Sift together the flour, and 3/4 cup of the sugar, set aside.
2. In a large bowl, whip the egg whites along with the vanilla, cream of tartar and salt, to medium stiff peaks. Gradually add the remaining sugar while continuing to whip to stiff peaks. When the egg white mixture has reached its maximum volume, fold in the sifted ingredients gradually, one third at a time. Do not overmix. Put the batter into the tube pan.

3. Bake for 40 to 45 minutes in the preheated oven, until the cake springs back when touched. Balance the tube pan upside down on the top of a bottle, to prevent decompression while cooling. When cool, run a knife around the edge of the pan and invert onto a plate.

ITALIAN CREAM CHEESE AND RICOTTA CHEESECAKE

Servings: 8 | Prep: 15m | Cooks: 2h | Total: 6h15m | Additional: 4h

NUTRITION FACTS

Calories: 703 | Carbohydrates: 49.8g | Fat: 50.1g | Protein: 16.1g | Cholesterol: 228mg

INGREDIENTS

- 2 (8 ounce) packages cream cheese, softened
- 1 teaspoon vanilla extract
- 1 (16 ounce) container ricotta cheese
- 3 tablespoons cornstarch
- 1 1/2 cups white sugar
- 3 tablespoons flour
- 4 eggs
- 1/2 cup butter, melted and cooled
- 1 tablespoon lemon juice
- 1 pint sour cream

DIRECTIONS

1. Preheat oven to 350 degrees F (175 degrees C). Lightly grease a 9-inch springform pan.
2. Mix the cream cheese and ricotta cheese together in a mixing bowl until well combined. Stir in the sugar, eggs, lemon juice, vanilla, cornstarch, flour, and butter. Add the sour cream last and stir. Pour the mixture into the prepared springform pan.
3. Bake in the preheated oven 1 hour; turn oven off and leave in oven 1 hour more. Allow to cool completely in refrigerator before serving.

CHOCOLATE COOKIE CHEESECAKE

Servings: 14 | Prep: 30m | Cooks: 1h | Total: 11h | Additional: 9h30m

NUTRITION FACTS

Calories: 753 | Carbohydrates: 62.9g | Fat: 52g | Protein: 11.2g | Cholesterol: 174mg

INGREDIENTS

- 2 cups chocolate sandwich cookie crumbs

- 1 teaspoon vanilla extract
- 2 tablespoons butter, melted
- 4 eggs
- 1/4 cup packed brown sugar
- 1 1/2 cups chocolate sandwich cookie crumbs
- 1 teaspoon ground cinnamon
- 16 ounces sour cream
- 2 pounds cream cheese, softened
- 1/4 cup white sugar
- 1 1/4 cups white sugar
- 1 teaspoon vanilla extract
- 1/3 cup heavy whipping cream
- 1 cup heavy whipping cream
- 2 tablespoons all-purpose flour
- 1 1/2 cups semisweet chocolate chips
- 1 teaspoon vanilla extract

DIRECTIONS

1. Combine 2 cups cookie crumbs, melted butter, brown sugar, and cinnamon in a medium bowl; firmly press mixture evenly onto bottom and 1 inch up sides of a 10-inch springform pan. Bake at 350 degrees F (175 degrees C) for 5 minutes; set aside.
2. In a large bowl, beat cream cheese until smooth. Gradually mix in 1 1/4 cups sugar, 1/3 cup whipping cream, flour, and 1 teaspoon vanilla. Beat in eggs, one at a time, beating after each addition. Pour 1/3 of batter into prepared pan. Top with 1 1/2 cups cookie pieces; pour in remaining batter.
3. Bake at 350 degrees F (175 degrees C) for 45 minutes. Remove cake from oven. Combine sour cream, 1/4 cup sugar, and 1 teaspoon vanilla; spread evenly on cheesecake. Continue baking for 7 minutes. Turn oven off and leave in oven 30 minutes. Remove cheesecake, and let cool completely on a wire rack.
4. Combine 1 cup whipping cream and chocolate chips in a saucepan; stir over low heat until chocolate melts, and then stir in 1 teaspoon vanilla. Pour mixture over cheesecake while still warm. Refrigerate until serving time. Should be at least 8 hours for refrigerator time, remove about 1/2 hour to 1 hour before serving, remove ring from springform pan, decorate to choice and get out your fork!

CREAM FILLED CUPCAKES

Servings: 36 | Prep: 15m | Cooks: 20m | Total: 50m | Additional: 15m

NUTRITION FACTS

Calories: 196 | Carbohydrates: 26.9g | Fat: 9.4g | Protein: 1.9g | Cholesterol: 14mg

INGREDIENTS

- 3 cups all-purpose flour
- 1 cup vegetable oil
- 2 cups white sugar
- 1 teaspoon vanilla extract
- 1/3 cup unsweetened cocoa powder
- 1/4 cup butter
- 2 teaspoons baking soda
- 1/4 cup shortening
- 1 teaspoon salt
- 2 cups confectioners' sugar
- 2 eggs
- 1 pinch salt
- 1 cup milk
- 3 tablespoons milk
- 1 cup water
- 1 teaspoon vanilla extract

DIRECTIONS

1. Preheat oven to 375 degrees F (190 degrees C). Line 36 muffin cups with paper liners.
2. In a large bowl, mix together the flour, sugar, cocoa, baking soda and 1 teaspoon salt. Make a well in the center and pour in the eggs, 1 cup milk, water, oil and 1 teaspoon vanilla. Mix well. Fill each muffin cup half-full of batter.
3. Bake in the preheated oven for 15 to 20 minutes, or until a toothpick inserted into the center of the cake comes out clean. Allow to cool.
4. Make filling: In a large bowl, beat butter and shortening together until smooth. Blend in confectioners' sugar and pinch of salt. Gradually beat in 3 tablespoons milk and 1 teaspoon vanilla. beat until light and fluffy. Fill a pastry bag with a small tip. Push tip through bottom of paper liner to fill each cupcake.

PUMPKIN CRUNCH CAKE

Servings: 18 | Prep: 15m | Cooks: 1h | Total: 1h15m

NUTRITION FACTS

Calories: 412 | Carbohydrates: 47.2g | Fat: 23.6g | Protein: 5.2g | Cholesterol: 48mg

INGREDIENTS

- 1 (15 ounce) can pumpkin puree
- 1 teaspoon salt
- 1 (12 fluid ounce) can evaporated milk
- 1 (18.25 ounce) package yellow cake mix

- 4 eggs
- 1 cup chopped pecans
- 1 1/2 cups white sugar
- 1 cup margarine, melted
- 2 teaspoons pumpkin pie spice
- 1 (8 ounce) container frozen whipped topping, thawed

DIRECTIONS

1. Preheat oven to 350 degrees F (175 degrees C). Lightly grease one 9x13 inch baking pan.
2. In a large bowl, combine pumpkin, evaporated milk, eggs, sugar, pumpkin pie spice, and salt. Mix well, and spread into the prepared pan.
3. Sprinkle cake mix over the top of the pumpkin mixture, and pat down. Sprinkle chopped pecans evenly over the cake mix, then drizzle with melted margarine.
4. Bake for 60 to 80 minutes, or until done. Top with whipped topping when ready to serve.

OLD FASHIONED PINEAPPLE UPSIDE-DOWN CAKE

Servings: 12 | Prep: 25m | Cooks: 30m | Total: 1h | Additional: 5m

NUTRITION FACTS

Calories: 321 | Carbohydrates: 55g | Fat: 10.4g | Protein: 3.2g | Cholesterol: 85mg

INGREDIENTS

- 4 eggs
- 1 teaspoon baking powder
- 1/2 cup butter
- 1/4 teaspoon salt
- 1 cup packed light brown sugar
- 1 cup white sugar
- 1 (20 ounce) can sliced pineapple
- 1 tablespoon butter, melted
- 10 maraschino cherries, halved
- 1 teaspoon almond extract
- 1 cup sifted cake flour

DIRECTIONS

1. Preheat oven to 325 degrees F (165 degrees C).
2. In a 10-inch heavy skillet with a heat-resistant handle (I use a cast iron skillet), melt 1/2 cup butter over very low heat. Remove from heat, and sprinkle brown sugar evenly over pan. Arrange pineapple slices to cover bottom of skillet. Distribute cherries around pineapple; set aside.
3. Sift together flour, baking powder, and salt.

4. Separate the eggs into two bowls. In a large bowl, beat egg whites just until soft peaks form. Add granulated sugar gradually, beating well after each addition. Beat until medium-stiff peaks form. In a small bowl, beat egg yolks at high speed until very thick and yellow. With a wire whisk or rubber scraper, using an over-and-under motion, gently fold egg yolks and flour mixture into whites until blended. Fold in 1 tablespoon melted butter or margarine and almond extract. Spread batter evenly over pineapple in skillet.
5. Bake until surface springs back when gently pressed with fingertip and a toothpick inserted in the center comes out clean, about 30 to 35 minutes. Loosen the edges of the cake with table knife. Cool the cake for 5 minutes before inverting onto serving plate.

APPLE COFFEE CAKE

Servings: 8 | Prep: 20m | Cooks: 35m | Total: 55m

NUTRITION FACTS

Calories: 275 | Carbohydrates: 41.4g | Fat: 11g | Protein: 3.6g | Cholesterol: 47mg

INGREDIENTS

- cooking spray
- 1 cup all-purpose flour
- 1 tablespoon flour, or as needed
- 3/4 teaspoon ground cinnamon
- 1/4cup butter, softened
- 1/2 teaspoon baking soda
- 3/4 cup brown sugar
- 1/4teaspoon salt
- 1 large egg
- 2 cups diced Granny Smith apple
- 1/4cup sour cream
- 1/4 cup brown sugar
- 1/4cup vanilla yogurt
- 1/4 cup all-purpose flour
- 1 teaspoon vanilla extract
- 2 tablespoons butter
- 1/2 teaspoon ground cinnamon

DIRECTIONS

1. Preheat oven to 350 degrees F (175 degrees C). Spray an 8-inch square baking dish with cooking spray; dust with 1 tablespoon flour.

2. Beat 1/4 cup butter and 3/4 cup brown sugar together with an electric mixer in a large bowl until light and fluffy. The mixture should be noticeably lighter in color. Beat egg into butter mixture. Add sour cream, vanilla yogurt, and vanilla extract to the mixture; beat to integrate.
3. Stir 1 cup flour, 3/4 teaspoon cinnamon, baking soda, and salt together in a bowl; add to the butter mixture and beat to combine into a batter. Fold apples into the batter. Pour batter into prepared baking dish.
4. Mix 1/4 cup brown sugar, 1/4 cup flour, 2 tablespoons butter, and 1/2 teaspoon cinnamon together in a bowl using a fork to achieve a crumbly consistency; sprinkle over the top of the batter.
5. Bake in the preheated oven until a toothpick inserted into the center comes out clean, 35 to 40 minutes. Cool in the pan for 10 minutes before removing to cool completely on a wire rack.

CHOCOLATE SURPRISE CUPCAKES

Servings: 24 | Prep: 30m | Cooks: 25m | Total: 55m

NUTRITION FACTS

Calories: 265 | Carbohydrates: 38.5g | Fat: 12g | Protein: 3.2g | Cholesterol: 18mg

INGREDIENTS

- 3 cups all-purpose flour
- 2 tablespoons vinegar
- 2 cups white sugar
- 2 teaspoons vanilla extract
- 1/2 cup unsweetened cocoa powder
- 1 (8 ounce) package cream cheese, softened
- 1 teaspoon salt
- 1 egg
- 2 teaspoons baking soda
- 1/2 cup white sugar
- 2/3 cup vegetable oil
- 1/4 teaspoon salt
- 2 cups water
- 2 tablespoons vinegar
- 1 cup semisweet chocolate chips

DIRECTIONS

1. Preheat oven to 350 degrees F (175 degrees C). Line 24 muffin cups with paper liners.
2. In a large bowl, mix together flour, 2 cups sugar, cocoa, 1 teaspoon salt and baking soda. Stir in oil, water, vinegar and vanilla until blended. Pour mixture into prepared muffin cups, filling each 2/3 full.

3. To make the filling: In a medium bowl, beat together the cream cheese, egg, 1/2 cup sugar and 1/4 teaspoon salt until light and fluffy. Stir in chocolate chips. Drop a heaping teaspoonful of the cream cheese mixture into each cupcake. Bake in the preheated oven for 25 minutes. Allow to cool.

CHOCOLATE CAPPUCCINO CHEESECAKE

Servings: 12 | Prep: 30m | Cooks: 1h | Total: 4h | Additional: 2h30m

NUTRITION FACTS

Calories: 619 | Carbohydrates: 45.1g | Fat: 45g | Protein: 9g | Cholesterol: 157mg

INGREDIENTS

- 1 cup chocolate cookie crumbs
- 1 cup sour cream
- 1/4 cup butter, softened
- 1/4 teaspoon salt
- 2 tablespoons white sugar
- 2 teaspoons instant coffee granules dissolved in 1/4 cup hot water
- 1/4 teaspoon ground cinnamon
- 1/4 cup coffee flavored liqueur
- 3 (8 ounce) packages cream cheese, softened
- 2 teaspoons vanilla extract
- 1 cup white sugar
- 1 cup heavy whipping cream
- 3 eggs
- 2 tablespoons confectioners' sugar
- 8 (1 ounce) squares semisweet chocolate
- 2 tablespoons coffee-flavored liqueur
- 2 tablespoons whipping cream
- 1 (1 ounce) square semisweet chocolate

DIRECTIONS

1. Preheat oven to 350 degrees F (175 degrees C). Butter one 9 or 10 inch springform pan.
2. Combine the chocolate wafer crumbs, softened butter, 2 tablespoons white sugar, and the cinnamon. Mix well and press mixture into the buttered springform pan, set aside.
3. In a medium sized bowl beat the softened cream cheese until smooth. Gradually add 1 cup white sugar mixing until well blended. Add eggs, one at a time. Beat at low speed until very smooth.
4. Melt the 8 ounces semisweet chocolate with 2 tablespoons whipping cream in a pan or bowl set over boiling water, stir until smooth.
5. Add chocolate mixture to cream cheese mixture and blend well. Stir in sour cream, salt, coffee, 1/4 cup coffee liqueur, and vanilla; beat until smooth. Pour mixture into prepared pan.

6. Bake in the center of oven at 350 degrees F (175 degrees C) for 45 minutes. Center will be soft but will firm up when chilled. Do not over bake. Leave cake in oven with the heat turned off and the door ajar for 45 minutes. Remove cake from oven and chill for 12 hours. Just before serving top cake with mounds of flavored whipped cream and garnish with chocolate leaves. Yields 16 servings.
7. To Make Flavored Whipped Cream: Beat whipping cream until soft peaks form, then beat in confectioner's sugar and 2 tablespoons coffee liqueur.
8. To Make Chocolate Leaves: Melt 1 ounce semisweet chocolate in a pan or bowl set over boiling water, stir until smooth. Brush real non-toxic plant leaves (such as orange leaves) on one side with melted chocolate. Freeze until firm and then peel off leaves. Freeze chocolate leaves until needed.

LEMON-BUTTERMILK POUND CAKE WITH AUNT EVELYN'S LEMON GLAZ

Servings: 12 | Prep: 20m | Cooks: 1h | Total: 1h30m | Additional: 10m

NUTRITION FACTS

Calories: 630 | Carbohydrates: 91.9g | Fat: 27.2g | Protein: 6.8g | Cholesterol: 129mg

INGREDIENTS

- 2 1/2 cups white sugar
- 1 cup buttermilk
- 1 1/2 cups butter, softened
- 1 teaspoon lemon extrac
- 4 eggs
- 2 cups confectioners' sugar
- 3 1/2 cups all-purpose flour
- 1/4 cup lemon juice
- 1/2 teaspoon salt
- 2 tablespoons butter, softened
- 1/2 teaspoon baking soda
- 1 tablespoon lemon zest

DIRECTIONS

1. Preheat oven to 350 degrees F (175 degrees C). Grease and flour a fluted tube pan (such as Bundt).
2. Beat white sugar and 1 1/2 cups butter together in a bowl with an electric mixer until light and fluffy, about 10 minutes. Add eggs one at a time, thoroughly beating each egg into the butter mixture before adding the next
3. Sift flour, salt, and baking soda together in a bowl. Add 1/3 of the flour mixture to the butter mixture; mix well. Pour in 1/2 the buttermilk and beat until combined. Repeat adding the remaining flour mixture and buttermilk, beating well after each addition, and ending with the flour mixture. Stir lemon extract into batter. Pour batter into prepared tube pan.

4. Reduce oven temperature to 325 degrees F (165 degrees C).
5. Bake in the oven until a toothpick inserted into the center of the cake comes out clean, 60 to 75 minutes. Cool in the pan for 10 minutes before removing to a cake platter or plate.
6. Beat confectioner's sugar, lemon juice, 2 tablespoons butter, and lemon zest together in a bowl until glaze is smooth. Pour about half the glaze over the cake; let cool. Pour remaining glaze over the cake.

MELT IN YOUR MOUTH BLUEBERRY CAKE
Servings: 12 | Prep: 30m | Cooks: 1h | Total: 1h30m

NUTRITION FACTS

Calories: 206 | Carbohydrates: 29.2g | Fat: 8.8g | Protein: 3.2g | Cholesterol: 55mg

INGREDIENTS

- 1/2 cup butter
- 1/3 cup milk
- 1/2 cup white sugar
- 2 egg whites
- 1/4 teaspoon salt
- 1/4 cup white sugar
- 1 teaspoon vanilla extract
- 1 1/2 cups fresh blueberries
- 2 egg yolks
- 1 tablespoon all-purpose flour
- 1 1/2 cups all-purpose flour
- 1 tablespoon white sugar
- 1 teaspoon baking powder

DIRECTIONS

1. Preheat oven to 350 degrees F (175 degrees C). Grease and flour an 8 inch square pan.
2. Cream butter or margarine and 1/2 cup sugar until fluffy. Add salt and vanilla. Separate eggs and reserve the whites. Add egg yolks to the sugar mixture; beat until creamy.
3. Combine 1 1/2 cups flour and baking powder; add alternately with milk to egg yolk mixture. Coat berries with 1 tablespoon flour and add to batter.
4. In a separate bowl, beat whites until soft peaks form. Add 1/4 cup of sugar, 1 tablespoon at a time, and beat until stiff peaks form. Fold egg whites into batter. Pour into prepared pan. Sprinkle top with remaining 1 tablespoon sugar.
5. Bake for 50 minutes, or until cake tests done.

FUDGE TRUFFLE CHEESECAKE

Servings: 14 | Prep: 1h | Cooks: 5h | Total: 3h30m

NUTRITION FACTS

Calories: 552 | Carbohydrates: 51.4g | Fat: 35.9g | Protein: 10.6g | Cholesterol: 127mg

INGREDIENTS

- 1 1/2 cups vanilla wafer crumbs
- 3 (8 ounce) packages cream cheese, room temperature
- 1/2 cup confectioners' sugar
- 1 (14 ounce) can sweetened condensed milk
- 1/3 cup unsweetened cocoa powder
- 4 eggs
- 1/3 cup butter, softened
- 2 teaspoons vanilla extract
- 2 cups semi-sweet chocolate chips

DIRECTIONS

1. Preheat oven to 300 degrees F (150 degrees C).
2. In a large mixing bowl, mix together crushed vanilla wafers, confectioners' sugar, cocoa, and butter by hand. Press ingredients into a 9-inch springform pan.
3. In the top of a double boiler, melt the chocolate chips, making sure that they are very smooth.
4. In a large bowl, beat cream cheese until fluffy with an electric mixer. Gradually beat in condensed milk until smooth. Mix in melted chocolate, eggs, and vanilla. Beat with electric mixer on low speed until the ingredients are thoroughly blended. Pour the filling into the prepared crust.
5. Bake at 300 degrees F (150 degrees C) for 55 minutes. The cake will seem underbaked in the center, but will continue to cook after you remove it from the oven.
6. Allow to cool to room temperature, then refrigerate for several hours before serving.

PUMPKIN ROLL

Servings: 16 | Prep: 30m | Cooks: 30m | Total: 2h | Additional: 1h

NUTRITION FACTS

Calories: 203 | Carbohydrates: 26.3g | Fat: 9.8g | Protein: 3.5g | Cholesterol: 54mg

INGREDIENTS

- 3 eggs
- 1/2 cup chopped walnuts
- 1 cup white sugar

- confectioners' sugar for dusting
- 2/3 cup canned pumpkin
- 1 cup confectioners' sugar
- 3/4 cup all-purpose flour
- 3/4 teaspoon vanilla extract
- 1/2 teaspoon ground cinnamon
- 2 tablespoons butter, softened
- 1 teaspoon baking soda
- 8 ounces cream cheese

DIRECTIONS

1. Preheat oven to 375 degrees F (190 degrees C). Grease a 15x10x1 inch baking pan and line with parchment paper. Grease and flour the paper.
2. In a large bowl, beat eggs on high for five minutes. Gradually add white sugar and pumpkin. Add flour, cinnamon, and baking soda. Spread batter evenly in pan. Sprinkle walnuts evenly on top.
3. Bake at 375 degrees F (190 degrees C) for 15 minutes or until cake springs back when lightly touched. Immediately turn out onto a linen towel dusted with confectioners sugar. Peel off paper and roll cake up in the towel, starting with the short end. Cool.
4. To Make Filling: Mix confectioners sugar, vanilla, butter or margarine, and cream cheese together till smooth.
5. Carefully unroll the cake. Spread filling over cake to within 1 inch of edges. Roll up again. Cover and chill until serving. Dust with additional confectioners' sugar, if desired.

MOIST RED VELVET CUPCAKES

Servings: 20 | Prep: 30m | Cooks: 20m | Total: 50m

NUTRITION FACTS

Calories: 160 | Carbohydrates: 26g | Fat: 5.5g | Protein: 2.7g | Cholesterol: 31mg

INGREDIENTS

- 1/2 cup butter
- 1 1/2 teaspoons baking soda
- 1 1/2 cups white sugar
- 1 tablespoon distilled white vinegar
- 2 eggs
- 2 cups all-purpose flour
- 1 cup buttermilk
- 1/3 cup unsweetened cocoa powder
- 1 fluid ounce red food coloring
- 1 teaspoon salt

- 1 teaspoon vanilla extract

DIRECTIONS

1. Preheat oven to 350 degrees F (175 degrees C). Grease two 12 cup muffin pans or line with 20 paper baking cups.
2. In a large bowl, beat the butter and sugar with an electric mixer until light and fluffy. Mix in the eggs, buttermilk, red food coloring and vanilla. Stir in the baking soda and vinegar. Combine the flour, cocoa powder and salt; stir into the batter just until blended. Spoon the batter into the prepared cups, dividing evenly.
3. Bake in the preheated oven until the tops spring back when lightly pressed, 20 to 25 minutes. Cool in the pan set over a wire rack. When cool, arrange the cupcakes on a serving platter and frost with desired frosting.

APPLE BANANA CUPCAKES
Servings: 24 | Prep: 20m | Cooks: 25m | Total: 45m

NUTRITION FACTS

Calories: 151 | Carbohydrates: 22.3g | Fat: 6.3g | Protein: 1.8g | Cholesterol: 16mg

INGREDIENTS

- 2 cups all-purpose flour
- 1 1/4 cups white sugar
- 1 teaspoon baking soda
- 2 eggs
- 1 teaspoon salt
- 1 teaspoon vanilla extract
- 1/2 teaspoon ground cinnamon
- 1/4 cup buttermilk
- 1/2 teaspoon ground nutmeg
- 1 cup ripe bananas, mashed
- 2/3 cup shortening
- 2 apples - peeled, cored and shredded

DIRECTIONS

1. Preheat oven to 375 degrees F (190 degrees C). Grease and flour 24 muffin cups, or use paper liners. Sift together the flour, baking soda, salt, cinnamon, and nutmeg. Set aside.
2. In a large bowl, cream together the shortening and sugar until light and fluffy. Beat in the eggs one at a time, then stir in the vanilla and buttermilk. Beat in the flour mixture, mixing just until incorporated. Fold in the mashed bananas and shredded apples. Fill each muffin cup half full.

3. Bake in the preheated oven for 20 to 25 minutes, or until a toothpick inserted into the center comes out clean. Allow to cool.

VEGAN CUPCAKES

Servings: 18 | Prep: 10m | Cooks: 15m | Total: 25m

NUTRITION FACTS

Calories: 152 | Carbohydrates: 22.6g | Fat: 6.4g | Protein: 1.5g | Cholesterol: 0mg

INGREDIENTS

- 1 tablespoon apple cider vinegar
- 1/2 teaspoon baking soda
- 1 1/2 cups almond milk
- 1/2 teaspoon salt
- 2 cups all-purpose flour
- 1/2 cup coconut oil, warmed until liquid
- 1 cup white sugar
- 1 1/4 teaspoons vanilla extract
- 2 teaspoons baking powder

DIRECTIONS

1. Preheat oven to 350 degrees F (175 degrees C). Grease two 12 cup muffin pans or line with 18 paper baking cups.
2. Measure the apple cider vinegar into a 2 cup measuring cup. Fill with almond milk to make 1 1/2 cups. Let stand until curdled, about 5 minutes. In a large bowl, Whisk together the flour, sugar, baking powder, baking soda and salt. In a separate bowl, whisk together the almond milk mixture, coconut oil and vanilla. Pour the wet ingredients into the dry ingredients and stir just until blended. Spoon the batter into the prepared cups, dividing evenly.
3. Bake in the preheated oven until the tops spring back when lightly pressed, 15 to 20 minutes. Cool in the pan set over a wire rack. When cool, arrange the cupcakes on a serving platter. Frost with desired frosting.

SCRUMPTIOUS STRAWBERRY SHORTCAKE

Servings: 12 | Prep: 25m | Cooks: 20m | Total: 55m | Additional: 10m

NUTRITION FACTS

Calories: 344 | Carbohydrates: 35.2g | Fat: 21.1g | Protein: 4.5g | Cholesterol: 74mg

INGREDIENTS

- 3 cups all-purpose flour
- 2/3 cup heavy cream
- 1/4 cup white sugar
- 1 egg, beaten
- 4 teaspoons baking powder
- 3 cups sliced fresh strawberries
- 3/4 teaspoon cream of tartar
- 3 tablespoons white sugar
- 1 cup butter

DIRECTIONS

1. Preheat oven to 350 degrees F (175 degrees C).
2. In a large bowl, mix flour, 1/4 cup sugar, baking powder and cream of tartar. Cut in butter with pastry blender or two knives. Stir in cream and egg. Turn out onto a lightly floured surface and knead 2 minutes. Press into a half-inch thick sheet. Cut into squares. Place on baking sheets.
3. Bake in preheated oven 20 minutes, or until golden. Sprinkle 3 tablespoons sugar over sliced berries.
4. Let shortcakes cool before splitting and filling with sugared berries.

BEST MOIST CHOCOLATE CAKE

Servings: 12 | Prep: 10m | Cooks: 40m | Total: 50m

NUTRITION FACTS

Calories: 382 | Carbohydrates: 52.3g | Fat: 17.4g | Protein: 6g | Cholesterol: 49mg

INGREDIENTS

- 1 cup margarine
- 2 1/2 cups all-purpose flour
- 1 3/4 cups white sugar
- 6 tablespoons unsweetened cocoa powder
- 3 eggs
- 1 1/2 teaspoons baking soda
- 1 1/2 teaspoons vanilla extract
- 1 teaspoon salt
- 1 1/2 cups milk

DIRECTIONS

1. Preheat oven to 350 degrees F (175 degrees C). Grease and flour a 9x13 inch pan. Sift together the flour, cocoa, baking soda and salt. Set aside.

2. In a large bowl, cream together the margarine and sugar until light and fluffy. Beat in the eggs one at a time, then stir in the vanilla. Beat in the flour mixture alternately with the milk, mixing just until incorporated. Pour batter into prepared pan.
3. Bake in the preheated oven for 40 to 45 minutes, or until a toothpick inserted into the center of the cake comes out clean. Allow to cool.

MARGARITA CAKE

Servings: 12 | Prep: 10m | Cooks: 1h | Total: 1h20m | Additional: 10m

NUTRITION FACTS

Calories: 393 | Carbohydrates: 53.7g | Fat: 16g | Protein: 4g | Cholesterol: 63mg

INGREDIENTS

- 1 (18.25 ounce) package orange cake mix
- 1/4 cup tequila
- 1 (3.4 ounce) package instant vanilla pudding mix
- 2 tablespoons triple sec liqueur
- 4 eggs
- 1 cup confectioners' sugar
- 1/2 cup vegetable oil
- 1 tablespoon tequila
- 2/3 cup water
- 2 tablespoons triple sec liqueur
- 1/4 cup lemon juice
- 2 tablespoons lime juice

DIRECTIONS

1. Preheat oven to 350 degrees F (175 degrees C). Grease and flour a 10 inch Bundt pan.
2. In a large bowl combine cake mix, pudding mix, eggs, oil, water, lemon juice 1/4 cup tequila and 2 tablespoons triple sec. Beat for 2 minutes.
3. Pour batter into prepared pan. Bake in the preheated oven for 45 to 50 minutes, or until a toothpick inserted into the center of the cake comes out clean. Cool in pan for 10 minutes; remove to rack and pour glaze over cake while still warm.
4. To make the glaze: In a small bowl, combine confectioners' sugar with 1 tablespoon tequila, 2 tablespoons triple sec and 2 tablespoons lime juice. Mix until smooth.

INCREDIBLY DELICIOUS ITALIAN CREAM CAKE

Servings: 12 | Prep: 30m | Cooks: 35m | Total: 1h35m | Additional: 30m

NUTRITION FACTS

Calories: 774 | Carbohydrates: 98.1g | Fat: 40.5g | Protein: 8.2g | Cholesterol: 143mg

INGREDIENTS

- 1 cup buttermilk
- 2 cups all-purpose flour
- 1 teaspoon baking soda
- 8 ounces cream cheese
- 1/2 cup butter
- 1/2 cup butter
- 1/2 cup shortening
- 1 teaspoon vanilla extract
- 2 cups white sugar
- 4 cups confectioners' sugar
- 5 eggs
- 2 tablespoons light cream
- 1 teaspoon vanilla extract
- 1/2 cup chopped walnuts
- 1 cup flaked coconut
- 1 cup sweetened flaked coconut
- 1 teaspoon baking powder

DIRECTIONS

1. Preheat oven to 350 degrees F (175 degrees C). Grease three 9 inch round cake pans. In a small bowl, dissolve the baking soda in the buttermilk; set aside.
2. In a large bowl, cream together 1/2 cup butter, shortening and white sugar until light and fluffy. Mix in the eggs, buttermilk mixture, 1 teaspoon vanilla, 1 cup coconut, baking powder and flour. Stir until just combined. Pour batter into the prepared pans.
3. Bake in the preheated oven for 30 to 35 minutes, or until a toothpick inserted into the center of the cake comes out clean. Allow to cool.
4. To Make Frosting: In a medium bowl, combine cream cheese, 1/2 cup butter, 1 teaspoon vanilla and confectioners' sugar. Beat until light and fluffy. Mix in a small amount of cream to attain the desired consistency. Stir in chopped nuts and remaining flaked coconut. Spread between layers and on top and sides of cooled cake.

CHOCOLATE PUDDING FUDGE CAKE

Servings: 12 | Prep: 15m | Cooks: 40m | Total: 1h5mm | Additional: 10m

NUTRITION FACTS

Calories: 629 | Carbohydrates: 67.8g | Fat: 40.8g | Protein: 7.9g | Cholesterol: 88mg

INGREDIENTS

- 1 (18.25 ounce) package devil's food cake mix
- 1/2 cup water
- 1 (3.9 ounce) package instant chocolate pudding mix
- 4 eggs
- 1 cup sour cream
- 2 cups semisweet chocolate chips
- 1 cup milk
- 6 tablespoons butter
- 1/2 cup vegetable oil
- 1 cup semisweet chocolate chips

DIRECTIONS

1. Preheat oven to 350 degrees F (175 degrees C). Grease and flour a 10 inch Bundt pan.
2. In a large bowl, combine cake mix, pudding mix, sour cream, milk, oil, water and eggs. Beat for 4 minutes, then mix in 2 cups chocolate chips.
3. Pour batter into prepared pan. Bake in the preheated oven for 40 to 50 minutes, or until a toothpick inserted into the center of the cake comes out clean. Cool 10 minutes in the pan, then turn out onto a wire rack and cool completely.
4. To make the glaze: Melt the butter and 1 cup chocolate chips in a double boiler or microwave oven. Stir until smooth and drizzle over cake.

BLUEBERRY POUND CAKE

Servings: 16 | Prep: 20m | Cooks: 1h10m | Total: 1h30m

NUTRITION FACTS

Calories: 338 | Carbohydrates: 48.8g | Fat: 14.5g | Protein: 4.3g | Cholesterol: 81mg

INGREDIENTS

- 2 tablespoons butter
- 2 cups white sugar
- 1/4 cup white sugar
- 4 eggs
- 2 3/4 cups all-purpose flour
- 1 teaspoon vanilla extract
- 1 teaspoon baking powder
- 2 cups fresh blueberries
- 1/2 teaspoon salt
- 1/4 cup all-purpose flour

- 1 cup butter

DIRECTIONS

1. Preheat oven to 325 degrees F (165 degrees C). Grease a 10-inch tube pan with 2 tablespoons butter. Sprinkle pan with 1/4 cup sugar.
2. Mix together 2 3/4 cups flour, baking powder and salt. Set aside.
3. In a large bowl, cream together 1 cup butter and 2 cups sugar until light and fluffy. Beat in the eggs one at a time, then stir in the vanilla. Gradually beat in the flour mixture. Dredge blueberries with remaining 1/4 cup flour, then fold into batter.
4. Pour batter into the prepared pan.
5. Bake in the preheated oven for 70 to 80 minutes, or until a toothpick inserted into the center of the cake comes out clean. Let cool in pan for 10 minutes, then turn out onto a wire rack and cool completely.

PUMPKIN ROLL

Servings: 10 | Prep: 15m | Cooks: 25m | Total: 1h | Additional: 20m

NUTRITION FACTS

Calories: 289 | Carbohydrates: 42.2g | Fat: 11.8g | Protein: 4.7g | Cholesterol: 87mg

INGREDIENTS

- 3 eggs, beaten
- 2 tablespoons butter, softened
- 1 cup white sugar
- 8 ounces cream cheese
- 1/2 teaspoon ground cinnamon
- 1 cup confectioners' sugar
- 2/3 cup pumpkin puree
- 1/4 teaspoon vanilla extract
- 3/4 cup all-purpose flour
- confectioners' sugar for dusting
- 1 teaspoon baking soda

DIRECTIONS

1. Preheat oven to 375 degrees F (190 degrees C). Butter or grease one 10x15 inch jelly roll pan.
2. In a mixing bowl, blend together the eggs, sugar, cinnamon, and pumpkin. In a separate bowl, mix together flour and baking soda. Add to pumpkin mixture and blend until smooth. Evenly spread the mixture over the prepared jelly roll pan.
3. Bake 15 to 25 minutes in the preheated oven. Remove from oven and allow to cool enough to handle.

4. Remove cake from pan and place on tea towel (cotton, not terry cloth). Roll up the cake by rolling a towel inside cake and place seam side down to cool.
5. Prepare the frosting by blending together the butter, cream cheese, confectioners sugar, and vanilla.
6. When cake is completely cooled, unroll and spread with cream cheese filling. Roll up again without towel. Wrap with plastic wrap and refrigerate until ready to serve. Sprinkle top with confectioners sugar and slice into 8-10 servings.

CHEESE CAKE CUPS
Servings: 16 | Prep: 15m | Cooks: 15m | Total: 30m

NUTRITION FACTS

Calories: 172 | Carbohydrates: 14.5g | Fat: 11.5g | Protein: 3.2g | Cholesterol: 54mg

INGREDIENTS

- 16 vanilla wafer cookies
- 2 eggs
- 2 (8 ounce) packages cream cheese, softened
- 1 teaspoon vanilla extract
- 3/4 cup white sugar

DIRECTIONS

1. Preheat oven to 350 degrees F (175 degrees C). Line muffin pans with cupcake papers.
2. Place one wafer cookie in the bottom of each cupcake paper. In a medium bowl, cream together cream cheese and sugar. Beat in eggs and vanilla until smooth. Pour over wafers in cupcake papers.
3. Bake in preheated oven 15 minutes, until golden and set.

LEMON CAKE
Servings: 20 | Prep: 15m | Cooks: 28m | Total: 43m

NUTRITION FACTS

Calories: 159 | Carbohydrates: 30g | Fat: 3.1g | Protein: 2g | Cholesterol: 1mg

INGREDIENTS

- 1 (18.25 ounce) package yellow cake mix
- 3/4 cup nonfat milk
- 1 (3.4 ounce) package instant lemon pudding mix
- 1/2 teaspoon lemon extract
- 1 3/4 cups water
- 1 (1 ounce) package instant sugar-free vanilla pudding mix

- 3 egg whites
- 1 (8 ounce) container frozen light whipped topping, thawed

DIRECTIONS

1. Preheat oven to 350 degrees F (175 degrees C). Spray a 10x15 inch pan with non-stick cooking spray.
2. In a large bowl, mix together cake mix and lemon pudding mix. Pour in water and egg whites. Beat on low speed for 1 minute. Increase speed to high and beat for 4 minutes. Pour batter into prepared 10x15 inch pan.
3. Bake in the preheated oven for 25 to 30 minutes, or until a toothpick inserted into the center of the cake comes out clean. Allow to cool completely.
4. In a large bowl, combine milk, lemon extract and vanilla pudding mix. Beat on low for 2 minutes. Fold in whipped topping. Spread over cooled cake. Store cake in refrigerator.

APPLE HARVEST POUND CAKE WITH CARAMEL GLAZE

Servings: 12 | Prep: 30m | Cooks: 1h20m | Total: 1h50m

NUTRITION FACTS

Calories: 682 | Carbohydrates: 71.1g | Fat: 42.8g | Protein: 6.5g | Cholesterol: 67mg

INGREDIENTS

- 2 cups white sugar
- 1 teaspoon salt
- 1 1/2 cups vegetable oil
- 2 medium Granny Smith apples - peeled, cored and chopped
- 2 teaspoons vanilla extract
- 1 cup chopped walnuts
- 3 eggs
- 1/2 cup butter or margarine
- 3 cups all-purpose flour
- 2 teaspoons milk
- 1 teaspoon baking soda
- 1/2 cup brown sugar
- 1/2 teaspoon ground cinnamon

DIRECTIONS

1. Preheat the oven to 350 degrees F (175 degrees C). Grease a 9 inch Bundt pan.
2. In a large bowl, beat the sugar, oil, vanilla and eggs with an electric mixer until light and fluffy. Combine the flour, baking soda, cinnamon and salt; stir into the batter just until blended. Fold in the apples and walnuts using a spoon. Pour into the prepared pan.

3. Bake for 1 hour and 20 minutes in the preheated oven, until a toothpick inserted into the crown or the cake comes out clean. Allow to cool for about 20 minutes then invert on to a wire rack.
4. Make the glaze by heating the butter, milk and brown sugar in a small saucepan over medium heat. Bring to a boil, stirring to dissolve the sugar, then remove from the heat. Drizzle over the warm cake. I like to place a sheet of aluminum foil under the cooling rack to catch the drips for easy clean up.

WHITE TEXAS SHEET CAKE

Servings: 24 | Prep: 20m | Cooks: 20m | Total: 40m | Additional: 20m

NUTRITION FACTS

Calories: 344 | Carbohydrates: 48.1g | Fat: 16.7g | Protein: 2.4g | Cholesterol: 48mg

INGREDIENTS

- 1 cup butter
- 1/2 teaspoon salt
- 1 cup water
- 1 teaspoon baking soda
- 2 cups all-purpose flour
- 1/2 cup butter
- 2 cups white sugar
- 1/4 cup milk
- 2 eggs
- 4 1/2 cups confectioners' sugar
- 1/2 cup sour cream
- 1/2 teaspoon almond extract
- 1 teaspoon almond extract
- 1 cup chopped pecans

DIRECTIONS

1. Preheat oven to 375 degrees F (190 degrees C).
2. In a large saucepan, bring 1 cup butter and water to a boil. Remove from heat, and stir in flour, sugar, eggs, sour cream, 1 teaspoon almond extract, salt, and baking soda until smooth. Pour batter into a greased 10x15-inch baking pan.
3. Bake in the preheated oven for 20 to 22 minutes, or until cake is golden brown and tests done. Cool for 20 minutes.
4. Combine 1/2 cup butter and milk in a saucepan; bring to a boil. Remove from heat. Mix in sugar, and 1/2 teaspoon almond extract. Stir in pecans. Spread frosting over warm cake.

THE BEST UNBAKED CHERRY CHEESECAKE EVER

Servings: 12 | Prep: 30m | Cooks: 2h | Total: 2h30m | Additional: 2h

NUTRITION FACTS

Calories: 296 | Carbohydrates: 30.7g | Fat: 18.5g | Protein: 2.6g | Cholesterol: 48mg

INGREDIENTS

- 1 1/4 cups graham cracker crumbs
- 1 cup powdered sugar
- 1/4 cup margarine, softened
- 1 teaspoon vanilla extract
- 1/4 cup sugar
- 1 cup heavy cream, whipped
- 1 (8 ounce) package cream cheese
- 1 (12.5 ounce) can cherry pie filling (or other filling of your choice)

DIRECTIONS

1. Mix together graham cracker crumbs, margarine, and sugar in a bowl until well incorporated and crumbly. Press into a pie plate, going up the sides as much as possible.
2. Beat together the cream cheese, sugar, and vanilla in a bowl until smooth and spreadable. Whisk whipped cream into cream cheese mixture until smooth. Pour cream cheese into prepared crust. Smooth the top with a spatula, and refrigerate until firm, about 2 to 3 hours. Spread the cherry pie filling over the top, and refrigerate until serving.

BANANA PUDDING CAKE

Servings: 12 | Prep: 30m | Cooks: 1h | Total: 2h | Additional: 30m

NUTRITION FACTS

Calories: 404 | Carbohydrates: 65.3g | Fat: 14.6g | Protein: 5g | Cholesterol: 63mg

INGREDIENTS

- 1 (18.25 ounce) package yellow cake mix
- 3/4 cup mashed bananas
- 1 (3.5 ounce) package instant banana pudding mix
- 2 cups confectioners' sugar
- 4 eggs
- 2 tablespoons milk
- 1 cup water
- 1 dash vanilla extract

- 1/4 cup vegetable oil
- 1/2 cup chopped walnuts (optional)

DIRECTIONS

1. Preheat oven to 350 degrees F (175 degrees C). Grease and flour a 10 inch Bundt pan.
2. In a large bowl, stir together cake mix and pudding mix. Make a well in the center and pour in eggs, water, oil and mashed banana. Beat on low speed until blended. Scrape bowl, and beat 4 minutes on medium speed. Pour batter into prepared pan.
3. Bake in a preheated oven for 50 to 55 minutes, or until cake tests done. Let cool in pan for 10 minutes, then turn out onto a wire rack and cool completely.
4. To make glaze: In a small bowl, combine confectioners' sugar, milk and vanilla. Whisk until smooth and of a drizzling consistency. When cake is cooled, drizzle icing over cake with a zigzag motion. Sprinkle chopped nuts over wet icing if desired.

APPLE BUNDT CAKE

Servings: 12 | Prep: 30m | Cooks: 1h | Total: 2h | Additional: 30m

NUTRITION FACTS

Calories: 523 | Carbohydrates: 66.3g | Fat: 26.7g | Protein: 6.9g | Cholesterol: 62mg

INGREDIENTS

- 2 cups apples - peeled, cored and diced
- 1 cup vegetable oil
- 1 tablespoon white sugar
- 1/4 cup orange juice
- 1 teaspoon ground cinnamon
- 2 1/2 teaspoons vanilla extract
- 3 cups all-purpose flour
- 4 eggs
- 3 teaspoons baking powder
- 1 cup chopped walnuts
- 1/2 teaspoon salt
- 1/4 cup confectioners' sugar for dusting
- 2 cups white sugar

DIRECTIONS

1. Preheat oven to 350 degrees F (175 degrees C). Grease and flour a 10 inch Bundt or tube pan. In a medium bowl, combine the diced apples, 1 tablespoon white sugar and 1 teaspoon cinnamon; set aside. Sift together the flour, baking powder and salt; set aside.

2. In a large bowl, combine 2 cups white sugar, oil, orange juice, vanilla and eggs. Beat at high speed until smooth. Stir in flour mixture. Fold in chopped walnuts.
3. Pour 1/3 of the batter into prepared pan. Sprinkle with 1/2 of the apple mixture. Alternate layers of batter and filling, ending with batter.
4. Bake in preheated oven for 55 to 60 minutes, or until the top springs back when lightly touched. Let cool in pan for 10 minutes, then turn out onto a wire rack and cool completely. Sprinkle with confectioners' sugar.

AUNT JOHNNIE'S POUND CAKE

Servings: 12 | Prep: 30m | Cooks: 1h30m | Total: 2h

NUTRITION FACTS

Calories: 544 | Carbohydrates: 70.8g | Fat: 26.7g | Protein: 6.4g | Cholesterol: 120mg

INGREDIENTS

- 1/2 cup shortening
- 2 teaspoons almond extract
- 1 cup butter
- 1 cup milk
- 2 1/2 cups white sugar
- 1/2 teaspoon baking powder
- 5 eggs
- 3 cups cake flour

DIRECTIONS

1. Preheat oven to 300 degrees F (150 degrees C). Lightly grease and flour a 10 inch Bundt pan.
2. Cream shortening, butter and sugar until light and fluffy (for best results use an electric mixer). This will take a while. Add eggs one at a time, beating well after each addition. Beat in almond extract.
3. Combine baking powder and flour. Stir into creamed mixture alternately with the milk, starting and ending with flour. Pour batter into prepared pan.
4. Bake in the preheated oven for 1 to 1 1/2 hours, or until a toothpick inserted into the center of the cake comes out clean. Let cool in pan for 10 minutes, then turn out onto a wire rack and cool completely.

BUCHE DE NOEL

Servings: 12 | Prep: 45m | Cooks: 15m | Total: 1h30m | Additional: 30m

NUTRITION FACTS

Calories: 276 | Carbohydrates: 27.6g | Fat: 17.7g | Protein: 5.1g | Cholesterol: 157mg

INGREDIENTS

- 2 cups heavy cream
- 1/3 cup unsweetened cocoa powder
- 1/2 cup confectioners' sugar
- 1 1/2 teaspoons vanilla extract
- 1/2 cup unsweetened cocoa powder
- 1/8 teaspoon salt
- 1 teaspoon vanilla extract
- 6 egg whites
- 6 egg yolks
- 1/4 cup white sugar
- 1/2 cup white sugar
- confectioners' sugar for dusting

DIRECTIONS

1. Preheat oven to 375 degrees F (190 degrees C). Line a 10x15 inch jellyroll pan with parchment paper. In a large bowl, whip cream, 1/2 cup confectioners' sugar, 1/2 cup cocoa, and 1 teaspoon vanilla until thick and stiff. Refrigerate.
2. In a large bowl, use an electric mixer to beat egg yolks with 1/2 cup sugar until thick and pale. Blend in 1/3 cup cocoa, 1 1/2 teaspoons vanilla, and salt. In large glass bowl, using clean beaters, whip egg whites to soft peaks. Gradually add 1/4 cup sugar, and beat until whites form stiff peaks. Immediately fold the yolk mixture into the whites. Spread the batter evenly into the prepared pan.
3. Bake for 12 to 15 minutes in the preheated oven, or until the cake springs back when lightly touched. Dust a clean dishtowel with confectioners' sugar. Run a knife around the edge of the pan, and turn the warm cake out onto the towel. Remove and discard parchment paper. Starting at the short edge of the cake, roll the cake up with the towel. Cool for 30 minutes.
4. Unroll the cake, and spread the filling to within 1 inch of the edge. Roll the cake up with the filling inside. Place seam side down onto a serving plate, and refrigerate until serving. Dust with confectioners' sugar before serving.

CHERRY CHEESECAKE

Servings: 12 | Prep: 30m | Cooks: 5h | Total: 5h30m | Additional: 5h

NUTRITION FACTS

Calories: 316 | Carbohydrates: 44.2g | Fat: 13.7g | Protein: 4.9g | Cholesterol: 32mg

INGREDIENTS

- 1 (9 inch) prepared graham cracker crust
- 1/3 cup lemon juice

- 1 (8 ounce) package cream cheese, softened
- 1 teaspoon vanilla extract
- 1 (14 ounce) can sweetened condensed milk
- 1 (21 ounce) can cherry pie filling

DIRECTIONS

1. Place softened cream cheese in a mixing bowl; add condensed milk, lemon juice, and vanilla. Beat until well blended. Pour mixture into the pie crust. Chill for 5 hours. DO NOT FREEZE!!!
2. Pour cherry pie filling on top of pie. Serve.

PUMPKIN MUFFINS WITH STREUSEL TOPPING

Servings: 18 | Prep: 30m | Cooks: 25m | Total: 55m

NUTRITION FACTS

Calories: 292 | Carbohydrates: 46.6g | Fat: 10.7g | Protein: 3.7g | Cholesterol: 34mg

INGREDIENTS

- 2 1/2 cups all-purpose flour
- 2/3 cup vegetable oil
- 1/2 cup rolled oats
- 1/2 cup applesauce
- 4 teaspoons pumpkin pie spice
- 3 eggs
- 2 teaspoons baking soda
- 1 teaspoon vanilla extract
- 1 teaspoon baking powder
- 1/4 cup raisins (optional)
- 1 teaspoon salt
- 1/4 cup packed brown sugar
- 1 1/2 cups pumpkin puree
- 2 tablespoons butter, softened
- 1 cup brown sugar
- 2 tablespoons rolled oats
- 1 cup white sugar
- 2 tablespoons all-purpose flour

DIRECTIONS

1. Preheat oven to 350 degrees F (175 degrees C). Grease or line 18 muffin cups with paper liners.

2. Combine 2 1/2 cups flour, 1/2 cup oats, pumpkin pie spice, baking soda, baking powder, and salt together in a bowl. Whisk pumpkin puree, 1 cup brown sugar, white sugar, vegetable oil, applesauce, eggs, and vanilla extract together in a separate large bowl. Stir flour mixture into pumpkin mixture; mix well. Fold in raisins.
3. Beat 1/4 cup brown sugar with butter in a bowl until creamy and smooth. Whisk 2 tablespoons oats and 2 tablespoons flour, using a fork, into sugar-butter mixture until streusel topping is crumbly.
4. Pour the batter into the prepared muffin tin. Sprinkle each muffin with streusel topping.
5. Bake in the preheated oven until a toothpick inserted in the center of a muffin comes out clean, 25 to 35 minutes.

COCONUT CREAM POUND CAKE

Servings: 16 | Prep: 15m | Cooks: 1h20m | Total: 1h35m

NUTRITION FACTS

Calories: 451 | Carbohydrates: 60.7g | Fat: 21.1g | Protein: 6.2g | Cholesterol: 116mg

INGREDIENTS

- 1 cup butter, softened
- 1 teaspoon coconut extract
- 1 (8 ounce) package cream cheese, softened
- 3 cups all-purpose flour
- 3 cups white sugar
- 1/2 teaspoon baking powder
- 6 eggs
- 2 cups flaked coconut

DIRECTIONS

1. Preheat the oven to 325 degrees F (165 degrees C). Grease and flour a 10 inch tube pan.
2. In a large bowl, cream together the butter and cream cheese until well blended. Add sugar, and beat until light and fluffy. Blend in the eggs one at a time, then stir in the coconut extract. Mix in flour and baking powder until just moistened, then stir in coconut. Spoon batter into the prepared pan.
3. Bake for 1 hour and 20 minutes in the preheated oven, until a knife inserted into the cake comes out clean. Allow the cake to cool in the pan for 10 minutes before inverting onto a cooling rack.

SURPRISE BANANA CAKE

Servings: 24 | Prep: 30m | Cooks: 30m | Total: 1h

NUTRITION FACTS

Calories: 144 | Carbohydrates: 21.2g | Fat: 6g | Protein: 2.2g | Cholesterol: 26mg

INGREDIENTS

- 1 cup white sugar
- 1 teaspoon baking soda
- 1/2 cup unsalted butter
- 1/2 teaspoon salt
- 2 eggs
- 1/2 cup chopped walnuts
- 4 ripe bananas, mashed
- 1 teaspoon vanilla extract
- 2 cups all-purpose flour

DIRECTIONS

1. Preheat oven to 375 degrees F (190 degrees C). Grease and flour one 9 x 13 inch cake pan.
2. Cream together the butter or margarine and the sugar.
3. Add eggs, bananas, flour, soda, salt, nuts, and vanilla. Mix thoroughly and pour batter into the prepared pan.
4. Bake at 375 degrees F (190 degrees C) for 30 minutes. Cool and frost cake.

RASPBERRY ALMOND COFFEECAKE

Servings: 10 | Prep: 30m | Cooks: 1h | Total: 1h30m

NUTRITION FACTS

Calories: 173 | Carbohydrates: 25.9g | Fat: 6.6g | Protein: 2.9g | Cholesterol: 30mg

INGREDIENTS

- 1 cup fresh raspberries
- 2 tablespoons butter, melted
- 3 tablespoons brown sugar
- 1 teaspoon vanilla extract
- 1 cup all-purpose flour
- 1 egg
- 1/3 cup white sugar
- 1/4 cup sliced almonds
- 1/2 teaspoon baking powder
- 1/4 cup sifted confectioners' sugar
- 1/4 teaspoon baking soda
- 1 teaspoon milk
- 1/8 teaspoon salt
- 1/4 teaspoon vanilla extract

- 1/2 cup sour cream

DIRECTIONS

1. Preheat oven to 350 degrees F (175 degrees C). Spray an 8 inch round cake pan with cooking spray.
2. Combine raspberries and brown sugar in a bowl. Set aside.
3. In a large bowl, combine flour, sugar, baking soda, baking powder, and salt. Combine sour cream, butter or margarine, 1 teaspoon vanilla, and egg, and add to flour mixture. Stir just until moist. Spoon 2/3 of the batter into the prepared pan. Spread raspberry mixture evenly over the batter. Spoon remaining batter over raspberry mixture. Top with almonds.
4. Bake for 40 minutes, or until a wooden pick inserted in center comes out clean. Let cool for 10 minutes on a wire rack.
5. Combine confectioners' sugar, milk, and 1/4 teaspoon vanilla. Stir well. Drizzle glaze over cake. Serve warm or at room temperature.

TIRAMISU CHEESECAKE

Servings: 12 | Prep: 30m | Cooks: 40m | Total: 5h | Additional: 3h50m

NUTRITION FACTS

Calories: 528 | Carbohydrates: 40.2g | Fat: 36.2g | Protein: 10.1g | Cholesterol: 188mg

INGREDIENTS

- 1 (12 ounce) package ladyfingers
- 1 cup white sugar
- 1/4 cup butter, melted
- 2 eggs
- 1/4 cup coffee-flavored liqueur, divided
- 1/4 cup all-purpose flour
- 3 (8 ounce) packages cream cheese
- 1 (1 ounce) square semisweet chocolate
- 1 (8 ounce) container mascarpone cheese

DIRECTIONS

1. Preheat oven to 350 degrees F (175 degrees C). Place a pan of water on the bottom of the oven.
2. Crush the package of ladyfingers to fine crumbs. Mix the melted butter into the crumbs. Moisten with 2 tablespoons of the coffee liqueur. Press into an 8-inch springform pan.
3. In a large bowl, mix cream cheese, mascarpone, and sugar until very smooth. Add 2 tablespoons coffee liqueur, and mix. Add the eggs and the flour; mix slowly just until smooth. Pour batter over crust in the springform pan.

4. Place pan on middle rack of oven. Bake until just set, 40 to 45 minutes. Open oven door, and turn off the heat. Leave cake to cool in oven for 20 minutes. Remove from oven, and let it finish cooling, about 30 minutes. Refrigerate for at least 3 hours, or overnight.
5. Grate semisweet chocolate over the top right before serving.

MOIST CARROT CAKE

Servings: 12 | Prep: 30m | Cooks: 40m | Total: 1h20m | Additional: 10m

NUTRITION FACTS

Calories: 569 | Carbohydrates: 59.4g | Fat: 35.7g | Protein: 5.9g | Cholesterol: 62mg

INGREDIENTS

- 2 cups all-purpose flour
- 1 1/2 cups vegetable oil
- 2 teaspoons baking powder
- 2 cups white sugar
- 1 1/2 teaspoons baking soda
- 2 3/4 cups shredded carrots
- 1 teaspoon salt
- 1 (8 ounce) can crushed pineapple, drained
- 2 1/2 teaspoons ground cinnamon
- 3/4 cup chopped walnuts
- 4 eggs
- 1 cup flaked coconut

DIRECTIONS

1. Preheat oven to 325 degrees F (165 degrees C). Grease and flour a 9x13 inch pan. Mix together the flour, baking powder, baking soda, salt and cinnamon. Set aside.
2. In a large bowl, mix sugar, oil, and eggs. Beat in flour mixture. Stir in shredded carrots, crushed pineapple, chopped nuts and flaked coconut. Pour into prepared pan.
3. Bake in the preheated oven for 35 to 40 minutes, or until a toothpick inserted into the center of the cake comes out clean. Allow to cool.

TRES LECHES CAKE

Servings: 8 | Prep: 25m | Cooks: 45m | Total: 2h30m | Additional: 1h20m

NUTRITION FACTS

Calories: 642 | Carbohydrates: 75g | Fat: 33g | Protein: 14.2g | Cholesterol: 241mg

INGREDIENTS

- 1 cup white sugar
- 1 1/2 teaspoons baking powder
- 5 egg yolks
- 1 (14 ounce) can sweetened condensed milk
- 5 egg whites
- 1 (12 fluid ounce) can evaporated milk
- 1/3 cup milk
- 1 pint heavy whipping cream
- 1 teaspoon vanilla extract
- 10 maraschino cherries
- 1 cup all-purpose flour

DIRECTIONS

1. Preheat oven to 350 degrees F (175 degrees C). Butter and flour bottom of a 9-inch springform pan.
2. Beat the egg yolks with 3/4 cup sugar until light in color and doubled in volume. Stir in milk, vanilla, flour and baking powder.
3. In a small bowl, beat egg whites until soft peaks form. Gradually add remaining 1/4 cup sugar. Beat until firm but not dry. Fold 1/3 of the egg whites into the yolk mixture to lighten it; fold in remaining egg whites. Pour batter into prepared pan.
4. Bake in preheated oven for 45 to 50 minutes or until cake tester inserted into the middle comes out clean. Allow to cool 10 minutes.
5. Loosen edge of cake with knife before removing side of pan. Cool cake completely on a wire rack.
6. Place cooled cake on a deep serving plate. Use a two-pronged meat fork or a cake tester to pierce the surface of cake.
7. Mix together condensed milk, evaporated milk and 1/4 cup of the whipping cream. Set aside 1 cup of the measured milk mixture and refrigerate for another use. Pour remaining milk mixture over cake slowly until absorbed. Whip the remaining whipping cream until it thickens and reaches spreading consistency. Frost cake with whipped cream and garnish with cherries. Store cake in the refrigerator.

PEANUT BUTTER CUPCAKES

Servings: 24 | Prep: 10m | Cooks: 12m | Total: 22m

NUTRITION FACTS

Calories: 209 | Carbohydrates: 24.8g | Fat: 10.5g | Protein: 5.1g | Cholesterol: 17mg

INGREDIENTS

- 2 cups brown sugar
- 1 teaspoon vanilla extract

- 1/2 cup shortening
- 2 1/2 cups all-purpose flour
- 1 cup peanut butter
- 1 teaspoon baking soda
- 2 eggs
- 2 teaspoons cream of tartar
- 1 1/2 cups milk
- 1 pinch salt

DIRECTIONS

1. Preheat the oven to 350 degrees F (175 degrees C). Line a cupcake pan with paper liners, or grease and flour cups.
2. In a large bowl, mix together the brown sugar, shortening and peanut butter until light and fluffy. Beat in the eggs one at a time, then stir in the vanilla. Combine the flour, cream of tartar, baking soda and salt; stir into the batter alternately with the milk. Spoon into the prepared muffin cups.
3. Bake for 15 to 20 minutes in the preheated oven, until the top of the cupcakes spring back when lightly pressed. Cool in the pan for at least 10 minutes before removing to a wire rack to cool completely.

MARDI GRAS KING CAKE

Servings: 16 | Prep: 1h | Cooks: 30m | Total: 4h30m | Additional: 3h

NUTRITION FACTS

Calories: 418 | Carbohydrates: 68.7g | Fat: 13.4g | Protein: 7.2g | Cholesterol: 47mg

INGREDIENTS

- 1 cup milk
- 1 cup packed brown sugar
- 1/4 cup butter
- 1 tablespoon ground cinnamon
- 2 (.25 ounce) packages active dry yeast
- 2/3 cup chopped pecans
- 2/3 cup warm water (110 degrees F/45 degrees C)
- 1/2 cup all-purpose flour
- 1/2 cup white sugar
- 1/2 cup raisins
- 2 eggs
- 1/2 cup melted butter
- 1 1/2 teaspoons salt
- 1 cup confectioners' sugar

- 1/2 teaspoon freshly grated nutmeg
- 1 tablespoon water
- 5 1/2 cups all-purpose flour

DIRECTIONS

1. Scald milk, remove from heat and stir in 1/4 cup of butter. Allow mixture to cool to room temperature. In a large bowl, dissolve yeast in the warm water with 1 tablespoon of the white sugar. Let stand until creamy, about 10 minutes.
2. When yeast mixture is bubbling, add the cooled milk mixture. Whisk in the eggs. Stir in the remaining white sugar, salt and nutmeg. Beat the flour into the milk/egg mixture 1 cup at a time. When the dough has pulled together, turn it out onto a lightly floured surface and knead until smooth and elastic, about 8 to 10 minutes.
3. Lightly oil a large bowl, place the dough in the bowl and turn to coat with oil. Cover with a damp cloth or plastic wrap and let rise in a warm place until doubled in volume, about 2 hours. When risen, punch down and divide dough in half.
4. Preheat oven to 375 degrees F (190 degrees C). Grease 2 cookie sheets or line with parchment paper.
5. To Make Filling: Combine the brown sugar, ground cinnamon, chopped pecans, 1/2 cup flour and 1/2 cup raisins. Pour 1/2 cup melted butter over the cinnamon mixture and mix until crumbly.
6. Roll dough halves out into large rectangles (approximately 10x16 inches or so). Sprinkle the filling evenly over the dough and roll up each half tightly like a jelly roll, beginning at the wide side. Bring the ends of each roll together to form 2 oval shaped rings. Place each ring on a prepared cookie sheet. With scissors make cuts 1/3 of the way through the rings at 1 inch intervals. Let rise in a warm spot until doubled in size, about 45 minutes.
7. Bake in preheated oven for 30 minutes. Push the doll into the bottom of the cake. Frost while warm with the confectioners' sugar blended with 1 to 2 tablespoons of water.

CHOCOLATE POUND CAKE

Servings: 16 | Prep: 30m | Cooks: 1h | Total: 1h30m

NUTRITION FACTS

Calories: 394 | Carbohydrates: 52.6g | Fat: 19.7g | Protein: 5.1g | Cholesterol: 104mg

INGREDIENTS

- 1 1/2 cups butter, softened
- 1 cup buttermilk
- 3 cups white sugar
- 2 cups all-purpose flour
- 5 eggs
- 3/4 cup unsweetened cocoa powder
- 2 teaspoons vanilla extract

- 1/2 teaspoon baking powder
- 2 teaspoons instant coffee granules dissolved in 1/4 cup hot water
- 1 teaspoon salt

DIRECTIONS

1. Preheat oven to 325 degrees F (165 degrees C). Grease and flour a 10 inch Bundt pan. Mix together the flour, cocoa, baking powder, and salt. Set aside.
2. In a large bowl, cream together the butter and sugar until light and fluffy. Beat in the eggs one at a time, then stir in the vanilla. Beat in the flour mixture alternately with the dissolved coffee and buttermilk. Pour batter into prepared pan.
3. Bake in the preheated oven for 60 to 70 minutes, or until a toothpick inserted into the center of the cake comes out clean. Let cool in pan for 20 minutes, then turn out onto a wire rack and cool completely.

PLUM BLUEBERRY UPSIDE DOWN CAKE

Servings: 12 | Prep: 30m | Cooks: 40m | Total: 1h10m

NUTRITION FACTS

Calories: 229 | Carbohydrates: 35.9g | Fat: 8.8g | Protein: 2.7g | Cholesterol: 17mg

INGREDIENTS

- 1 1/4 cups all-purpose flour
- 1 cup white sugar
- 1 1/2 teaspoons baking powder
- 1 egg
- 1/4 teaspoon salt
- 1 teaspoon vanilla extract
- 3 tablespoons margarine
- 3/4 cup milk
- 1/4 cup brown sugar
- 4 black plums, pitted and thinly sliced
- 1/3 cup margarine
- 3/4 cup blueberries

DIRECTIONS

1. Preheat oven to 350 degrees F (175 degrees C). Grease a 9 inch cake pan. Combine the flour, baking powder and salt. Set aside.
2. In the prepared pan, combine 3 tablespoons margarine and brown sugar. Place pan inside the preheated oven until the margarine melts and begins to bubble. Set aside. In a large bowl, cream

together the 1/3 cup margarine and 1 cup white sugar until light and fluffy. Beat in the egg, then stir in the vanilla. Beat in the flour mixture alternately with the milk, mixing just until incorporated.
3. Arrange plums around the edges of the prepared pan, overlapping slightly. Distribute the blueberries in the center. Pour batter into prepared pan, covering fruit completely. Bake in the preheated oven for 40 minutes, or until a toothpick inserted into the center of the cake comes out clean. Allow to cool 15 minutes before serving.

PECAN SOUR CREAM POUND CAKE

Servings: 12 | Prep: 30m | Cooks: 1h30m | Total: 2h20m | Additional: 20m

NUTRITION FACTS

Calories: 594 | Carbohydrates: 89.7g | Fat: 23.8g | Protein: 7.1g | Cholesterol: 142mg

INGREDIENTS

- 1/4 cup chopped pecans
- 6 eggs
- 3 cups cake flour
- 1 teaspoon vanilla extract
- 1/2 teaspoon salt
- 1 cup sour cream
- 1/4 teaspoon baking soda
- 1 cup confectioners' sugar
- 1 cup unsalted butter
- 3 tablespoons orange juice
- 3 cups white sugar
- 1 teaspoon vanilla extract

DIRECTIONS

1. Preheat oven to 300 degrees F (150 degrees C). Grease and flour a 10 inch Bundt or tube pan. Sprinkle pecans on bottom of pan; set aside. Sift together flour, salt, and baking soda into a medium bowl; set aside.
2. In a large bowl, cream butter and white sugar until light and fluffy. Beat in eggs one at a time, then stir in vanilla. Add flour mixture alternately with sour cream. Pour batter over pecans in prepared pan.
3. Bake in the preheated oven for 75 to 90 minutes, or until a toothpick inserted into the center of the cake comes out clean. Let cool in pan for 20 minutes, then turn out onto a wire rack and cool completely.
4. To prepare the glaze: In a small bowl, combine confectioners' sugar, orange juice and 1 teaspoon vanilla. Drizzle over cake while still warm.

LEMON BUNDT CAKE

Servings: 12 | Prep: 15m | Cooks: 45m | Total: 1h

NUTRITION FACTS

Calories: 364 | Carbohydrates: 41.5g | Fat: 20.4g | Protein: 4.7g | Cholesterol: 73mg

INGREDIENTS

- 1 (18.25 ounce) package lemon cake mix
- 4 eggs
- 1 (3.4 ounce) package instant lemon pudding mix
- 1 cup lemon-lime flavored carbonated beverage
- 3/4 cup vegetable oil

DIRECTIONS

1. Preheat oven to 325 degrees F (165 degrees C). Grease and flour a 10-inch Bundt pan.
2. In a large bowl, combine cake mix and pudding mix, then stir in the oil. Beat in the eggs, one at a time, then stir in the lemon-lime soda.
3. Pour batter into prepared pan. Bake in the preheated oven for 45 to 50 minutes, or until a toothpick inserted into the center of the cake comes out clean. Allow to cool.

MINI CHEESECAKES WITH VANILLA WAFERS

Servings: 48 | Prep: 15m | Cooks: 15m | Total: 1h | Additional: 30m

NUTRITION FACTS

Calories: 95 | Carbohydrates: 11.8g | Fat: 4.8g | Protein: 1.3g | Cholesterol: 18mg

INGREDIENTS

- 1 (12 ounce) package vanilla wafers
- 2 eggs
- 2 (8 ounce) packages cream cheese
- 1 teaspoon vanilla extract
- 3/4 cup white sugar
- 1 (21 ounce) can cherry pie filling

DIRECTIONS

1. Preheat oven to 350 degrees F (175 degrees C). Line miniature muffin tins (tassie pans) with miniature paper liners.
2. Crush the vanilla wafers and place 1/2 tablespoon of the crushed vanilla wafers into the paper lined miniature muffin tins.

3. Cream together with an electric mixer the cream cheese, sugar, eggs and vanilla. Fill each miniature muffin liner with this mixture, almost to the top.
4. Bake at 350 degrees F (175 degrees C) for 15 minutes. Cool and then top with a teaspoonful of cherry (or any other flavor) pie filling.

AMARETTO CAKE

Servings: 12 | Prep: 30m | Cooks: 1h | Total: 1h30m

NUTRITION FACTS

Calories: 425 | Carbohydrates: 61.4g | Fat: 15.9g | Protein: 4g | Cholesterol: 63mg

INGREDIENTS

- 1 (18.25 ounce) package yellow cake mix
- 1/2 cup vegetable oil
- 4 eggs
- 1/4 teaspoon almond extract
- 1 (5.1 ounce) package instant vanilla pudding mix
- 1/2 cup amaretto liqueur
- 2 tablespoons amaretto liqueur
- 1 cup sifted confectioners' sugar
- 1/2 cup water

DIRECTIONS

1. Preheat oven to 350 degrees F (175 degrees C). Grease and flour a 10 inch Bundt pan.
2. In a large bowl, combine cake mix, eggs, instant vanilla pudding, water, oil, almond extract, and 2 tablespoons of the amaretto; blend together well. Pour batter into the prepared pan.
3. Bake in preheated oven for 40 to 45 minutes, or until a toothpick inserted into the center of cake comes out clean. Remove cake from oven and while it is still warm, poke holes in the surface. Drizzle with the Amaretto Glaze, insuring that some of the glaze fills the holes. Let the cake cool for at least 2 hours before removing from the pan.
4. To make Amaretto Glaze: Sift the confectioners' sugar, and combine it with the remaining 1/2 cup amaretto. Blend until smooth. You may add more amaretto as needed.

CHOCOLATE CAKE

Servings: 24 | Prep: 15m | Cooks: 35m | Total: 50m

NUTRITION FACTS

Calories: 162 | Carbohydrates: 26.6g | Fat: 5.8g | Protein: 2.5g | Cholesterol: 17mg

INGREDIENTS

- 2 cups all-purpose flour
- 1/2 cup vegetable oil
- 2 cups white sugar
- 1 cup milk
- 3/4 cup unsweetened cocoa powder
- 2 eggs
- 2 teaspoons baking soda
- 1 teaspoon vanilla extract
- 1 teaspoon baking powder
- 1 cup hot, strong coffee

DIRECTIONS

1. Preheat oven to 350 degrees F (175 degrees C). Grease and flour a 9x13 inch pan.
2. In a large bowl, stir together the flour, sugar, cocoa, baking powder, and baking soda. Add the oil, milk, eggs, and vanilla, mix until smooth. Stir in the hot coffee last. Spread evenly into the prepared pan.
3. Bake in the preheated oven for 25 to 35 minutes, or until a toothpick inserted into the cake comes out clean.

PEANUT BUTTER CAKE

Servings: 12 | Prep: 30m | Cooks: 30m | Total: 1h

NUTRITION FACTS

Calories: 696 | Carbohydrates: 81.1g | Fat: 38.7g | Protein: 11.5g | Cholesterol: 112mg

INGREDIENTS

- 1/2 cup creamy peanut butter
- 1 cup peanut butter
- 1/2 cup butter, softened
- 1/2 cup butter, softened
- 4 eggs
- 4 cups confectioners' sugar
- 1 (18.25 ounce) package butter cake mix
- 1/3 cup heavy cream
- 2/3 cup water

DIRECTIONS

1. Preheat oven to 325 degrees F (165 degrees C). Grease and flour two 9 inch round cake pans.

2. Combine 1/2 cup peanut butter and 1/2 cup butter or margarine. Cream until light and fluffy. Add eggs one at time, mixing well after each one. Add cake mix alternately with the water. Stir until just combined. Pour batter into prepared pans.
3. Bake at 325 degrees F (165 degrees C) for 25 minutes or until cake tests done. Allow cakes to cool in pan for 10 minutes and then turn out onto a cooling rack to cool completely. Assemble and frost with Peanut Butter Frosting once cool.
4. To Make Peanut Butter Frosting: Combine 1 cup peanut butter, and 1/2 cup butter or margarine cream together until light and fluffy. Add the confectioner's sugar. Mix in enough cream to make the frosting of a spreading consistency. Apply to cool cake.

APPLE CAKE

Servings: 24 | Prep: 30m | Cooks: 45m | Total: 1h30m | Additional: 15m

NUTRITION FACTS

Calories: 191 | Carbohydrates: 31.1g | Fat: 6.8g | Protein: 2.6g | Cholesterol: 25mg

INGREDIENTS

- 1 (18.25 ounce) package yellow cake mix
- 1 tablespoon all-purpose flour
- 3 eggs
- 1 tablespoon butter
- 1 (21 ounce) can apple pie filling
- 1 teaspoon ground cinnamon
- 3/4 cup packed brown sugar
- 1 cup chopped walnuts

DIRECTIONS

1. Preheat oven to 350 degrees F (175 degrees C). Grease and flour a 9x13 inch baking pan.
2. In a large bowl, mix together the cake mix, eggs and apple pie filling. Pour into the prepared pan. Combine the brown sugar, flour, butter, cinnamon and walnuts. Sprinkle over the top of the batter.
3. Bake in the preheated oven for 35 to 40 minutes, or until a toothpick inserted into the center of the cake comes out clean. Allow to cool.

OREO COOKIE CAKE

Servings: 24 | Prep: 30m | Cooks: 30m | Total: 1h | Additional: 30m

NUTRITION FACTS

Calories: 312 | Carbohydrates: 31.2g | Fat: 20g | Protein: 3.6g | Cholesterol: 32mg

INGREDIENTS

- 1 (20 ounce) package chocolate sandwich cookies
- 1 cup confectioners' sugar
- ½ cup butter
- 2 cups milk
- 1 (16 ounce) container frozen whipped topping, thawed
- 1 (3.5 ounce) package instant vanilla pudding mix
- 2 (8 ounce) packages cream cheese

DIRECTIONS

1. Crush cookies into bite size pieces. Reserve 1 cup for top. Melt butter and mix with rest of cookies. Press into 9x13 pan. Put in freezer for 5 minutes.
2. Blend 1/2 of the whipped topping, all of the cream cheese and confectioners' sugar. Spread over crust and place cake back in freezer.
3. Prepare instant pudding with the milk according to package directions then spread over top of cake. Spread the remaining whipped topping on top of the pudding then sprinkle with the remaining cookies. Keep cake refrigerated.

DOUBLE CHOCOLATE BROWNIE CAKE

Servings: 12 | Prep: 10m | Cooks: 1h | Total: 1h10m

NUTRITION FACTS

Calories: 501 | Carbohydrates: 56.8g | Fat: 29.3g | Protein: 7.5g | Cholesterol: 79mg

INGREDIENTS

- 1 (18.25 ounce) package devil's food cake mix
- 1/2 cup vegetable oil
- 1 (3.9 ounce) package instant chocolate pudding mix
- 1/2 cup water
- 4 eggs
- 2 cups semisweet chocolate chips
- 1 cup sour cream

DIRECTIONS

1. Preheat oven to 350 degrees F (175 degrees C). Grease and flour a 10 inch Bundt pan. Have all ingredients at room temperature.
2. In a large bowl, stir together cake mix and pudding mix. Make a well in the center and pour in eggs, sour cream, oil and water. Beat on low speed until blended. Scrape bowl, and beat 4 minutes on medium speed. Stir in chocolate chips. Pour batter into prepared pan.

3. Bake in the preheated oven for 50 to 60 minutes, or until a toothpick inserted into the center of the cake comes out clean. Allow to cool.

FRESH PINEAPPLE UPSIDE DOWN CAKE

Servings: 12 | Prep: 30m | Cooks: 30m | Total: 1h10m | Additional: 10m

NUTRITION FACTS

Calories: 290 | Carbohydrates: 41.3g | Fat: 13g | Protein: 3.6g | Cholesterol: 77mg

INGREDIENTS

- 3/4 cup butter
- 1/2 teaspoon salt
- 3/4 cup packed dark brown sugar
- 1/2 cup white sugar
- 3/4 cup unsweetened pineapple juice
- 3 eggs
- 1 1/2 cups all-purpose flour
- 1/2 teaspoon vanilla extract
- 2 teaspoons baking powder
- 1 fresh pineapple - peeled, cored and cut into rings

DIRECTIONS

1. Preheat oven to 400 degrees F (205 degrees C).
2. Melt the butter. Brush a little bit of the butter on the inside of a 9-inch cake pan.
3. Mix 5 tablespoons of the butter with the dark brown sugar and 1/4 cup of the pineapple juice. Place this mixture in the bottom of the cake pan. Arrange the pineapple rings on the brown sugar mixture in a decorative pattern (be creative). Set pan aside.
4. Stir together the flour, salt, white sugar, and baking powder.
5. Separate the eggs. Beat the whites until stiff but not dry.
6. Beat two of the egg yolks until lemony yellow. Stir in the remaining 1/2 cup pineapple juice, vanilla, and remaining melted butter. Add this mixture to the flour mixture. Gently fold in the egg whites. Pour batter over the top of the brown sugar and pineapple rings.
7. Bake in the preheated oven until cake springs back when lightly touched with a finger, about 30 minutes. Let cake cool in pan for 10 minutes then cover pan tightly with a serving dish and invert so that the pineapple side is up.